Chesty Puller and other War Heroes

Arnold Paulsen

Published by Trellis Publishing, 2021.

CHESTY PULLER AND OTHER WAR HEROES

First edition. July 11, 2021.

Copyright © 2021 Arnold Paulsen.

ISBN: 979-8224119486

Written by Arnold Paulsen.

CHESTY PULLER AND OTHER WAR HEROES

ARNOLD PAULSEN

The United States Marine Corps was founded in 1775 and have a very long and turbulent history. They are in charge of special missions that require outstanding tactics and were a part of every major conflict which involved the United States. Many men stood out since the founding of the Marine Corps, but Chesty Puller became a true legend. Puller was a fearless commander who led his men to numerous victories, but he was also reliable and caring. Puller was a true disciplinary who taught both the servicemen and their officers how to treat each other with respect. He was tough and enjoyed challenges that were put in front of him on battlefields. The tales about his accomplishments are constantly revisited by the Marines, and even though some of them might be fictional, everyone sits down to listen about the phenomenon called Chesty Puller.

Early life

Lewis Burwell "Chesty" Puller was born on June 26th, 1898 in West Point, Virginia. His parents were from a working-class background, and they taught the young Lewis to always try his hardest in order to succeed. Their names were Matthew and Martha Puller. Matthew worked in a grocery store while Martha stayed home and took care of the family. Puller's grandfather fought for the Confederacy and was a veteran of the American Civil War. Not to forget that General George S. Patton was his second cousin. Puller grew up in the wilderness, hunting, and fishing. He was also an avid reader, interested in military books. Puller would read them all the time, devouring a title after a title. His family was religious and were devoted Episcopalians. They taught the young Puller to have the same values. Unfortunately, Puller lost his father when he was only ten years old. He enjoyed listening to his father's tales of the American Civil War and was mesmerized by the effort of the men who were fighting in it. Puller wanted to be a part of something big as well and to show how courageous he was so he insisted to sign himself up to fight against Mexico in the well-known Border War of 1916. But his mother didn't want to send her teenage son into a conflict so he never got her permission.

Puller has already made up his mind about his future profession, and he enrolled in Virginia Military Institute in 1917. He was aware that he needed his military education but World War I was raging across the planet. Knowing that he might be more useful in the battle than in a classroom, Puller dropped out in August of 1918. His brief stint at Virginia Military School taught him a lot about the structure of the army and Puller was very impressed by the 5th Marine Regiment and their achievements in The Battle of Belleau Wood. Therefore, Lewis Puller decided to enlist in the United States Marine Corps. A long and difficult road laid in front of him but Lewis was prepared for it. He started out as a private and was sent to the Marine Corps Recruit Depot, Parris Island, South Carolina in order to go through the boot camp.

The World War I ended while Puller was still in training so he was never deployed to the battlefront. However, the interest in the Marine Corps grew every day, and they got plenty of new candidates who wanted to defend the country in any future conflict. Puller was recognized as one of the best privates at Marine Corps Recruit Depot, and his superiors encouraged him to attend Officer Candidates School at Quantico, Virginia. He graduated on June 16th, 1919 and immediately got the position of the second lieutenant. But the increase in the number of the Marines was staggering, and Puller received an inactive status just a couple of days after getting the promotion. Eager to serve his country, Puller decided to do something unusual and re-enlist hoping he would be in active duty again. He eventually received a corporal rank and endured the boot camp once again, training harder than ever before because he had envisioned the ultimate goal. His days were spent in physical activities which prepared him for any obstacles that were ahead of him. Puller's boot camp lasted for thirteen weeks and then he was notified that he would be shipped out for the first time. The excitement in him grew because he finally got his chance.

Shipping out to Haiti

As a corporate, Lewis Puller was sent to Haiti to join the Gendarmerie d'Haiti, and he was promoted to a lieutenant. Their mission was to fight the Caco Rebels who didn't agree with the United States and their meddling into the internal affairs of the country of Haiti. The government of Haiti had the full support of the United States back then, and the Gendarmerie d'Haiti was supposed to keep it that way. Of course, there were those who opposed the new leaders and were ready to do fight until the very end for their beliefs. Even though the whole situation was completely new to Puller, he did his job perfectly.

Puller was in Haiti for five years, and he engaged in fights with the rebels over forty times. He learned a lot during his stay, and that knowledge would be very valuable to Puller in the future. He led a small unit of soldiers who would engage with the rebels in the jungle and rough terrain. Puller got back to the United States in 1924, and he was once again promoted to the second lieutenant on March 6th, 1924. The Marine Corpse demanded that he complete several assignments in Norfolk and Quantico in Virginia which he passed with stellar results. Puller was then sent to the Marine Barracks at Pearl Harbor, Hawaii and afterward to San Diego, California in 1928.

Fighting in Nicaragua and the deployment after

After proving himself in Haiti, the Marines decided to send Puller on a similar mission to Nicaragua. He joined the Nicaraguan National Guard in December 1928. This is where Puller got his reputation as a fierce leader and commander who knew how to lead his men to the victory. Nicaragua was very similar to Haiti and Puller had an almost identical mission – fighting the rebels in the jungles. His first fight in Nicaragua led Puller's men to face a large group of heavily armed rebels who knew the terrain perfectly. But this didn't stop Puller to engage them. Puller was aware that the challenge was ahead of him and that the rebels are well-protected but he persisted. Puller's platoon shocked the rebels with their courage and persistence. They charged the impenetrable positions and won every single time. The fight lasted for over a week and Puller managed to repel the rebels and force them to move from that part of the jungle.

Puller was also a great tactician by then and was capable of thinking on the spot which was quite useful when his platoon was ambushed in the mountains of Nicaragua. The rebels were once again armed with machine guns and started shooting from all sides. Puller's platoon didn't expect the attack, and some of the soldiers didn't manage to find shelter in time. Four of them died right away. Puller ordered the rest of his people to find cover and start firing back. He then made a diversion and found a way to come up behind the rebels, resulting in another victory. There he earned a title of "The Tiger of the Mountains". In the end, Puller led five big battles against the rebels in Nicaragua and earned his first Navy Cross. He came home to the United States in 1933. Puller certainly made a name for himself during the time he spent in Nicaragua and Haiti. His fellow soldiers who had seen him in action would later testify that he was not afraid of anything, not even hand-to-hand combat. He didn't hesitate for a single moment and was capable of dealing with tough situations while keeping a cool head.

The Marines also recognized his fearlessness and after he came back home in 1939 Puller was sent to Beijing, China to serve with the Marines at American Legation. There he was in charge of training Chinese Marines, specifically their Horse Division who were training in order to break riots. Horseriding was not new to Puller and he excelled at this role as well. He didn't mind training with the Chinese Marines for hours and hours every day in order to help them learn how to attack a target while riding a horse. After that, Puller was assigned to USS Augusta which belonged to the Asiatic Fleet. Serving at sea was another challenge for Puller since he had never done it before and it was a good change of scenery for him. He came back to the United States once again in the summer of 1936, and he got a position of a teacher at The Basic School in Philadelphia. Puller was called back to the USS Augusta in 1939 where he continued to serve with the Marines on the ship. He then went to Shangai in 1940 where Puller was the commanding officer at 2nd Batallion, 4th Marines.

Puller was called back to the United States in 1941 where he was placed on a short leave. World War II was starting, and the States were not yet involved in a conflict. However, they recognized the possible threat and the military was on a stand-by. Puller became a commandant of 1st Battalion, 7th Marines of the 1st Marine Division and they were stationed at New River, North Carolina. Puller already had his famous nickname Chesty by then. Even though the origin of the nickname itself is a mystery and there are many versions of the story, it stuck with him for the rest of his life becoming a legend like a man himself. Some of his fellow Marines would later say that Puller got the nickname because of his enormous and visible chest. He was always standing straight, not hunching down for a second. One of the myths surrounding Chesty Puller was that he was shot and that the doctors placed a steel plate in his chest, making it even more prominent on his stature. Other Marines claimed that chesty is a saying they used for someone who was brave and cocky a bit which certainly could be applied to Puller who never backed down or showed weakness. And finally, some Marines said that he was always shouting orders as loud as he could and that is why his chest was always up.

When asked about the origins of his nickname, Chesty Puller wrote the following to his friend in 1954: *"I agree with you 100%. I had done a little soldiering previous to Guadalcanal and had been called a lot of names, but why 'Chesty'? Especially the steel part??"*

World War II

The attack on Pearl Harbour happened on December 7th, 1941 and it is a significant date for the history of the United States because it marked the start of the US involvement in the conflict. They were neutral while Germany invaded various European countries but this time the United States was directly affected by the war and they simply couldn't remain on the sidelines any longer. Chesty Puller and his Marines were deployed to Samoa on May 8th, 1942 as a part of 3rd Marine Brigade. They were there with a mission of defending the island during the early staged of the Pacific War. On September 4th, 1942 3rd Marine Brigade left for Guadalcanal and joined the 1st Division. This is where Chesty Puller and his men saw real battles. As soon as they arrived at Guadalcanal, the US Marines laid out a strategy which involved Puller's brigade. They were ordered to march around Mount Austen, go over the Matanikau River and take control of the area. The 1st Raider Battalion led by Lieutenant Colonel Samuel B. Griffith was supposed to scout the area of Tassafaronga to the west. The US Marines knew that there were Japanese forces on the island and they suspected there were around 400 of them stationed in that area.

However, the Japanese knew that the allies will be landing on Guadalcanal since the location was quite strategically important, and they sent a larger number of soldiers there in order to surprise them. Therefore, the US Marines didn't have the real information about the enemy troops in the area. The entire 124th Infantry Regiment which had 1,900 soldiers was on the island, as well as the Maizuru Battalion. There was a total of 4000 Japanese soldiers on Guadalcanal, and the US Marines didn't even know what they were getting into. Puller's battalion had around 930 men and they started marching towards the Mount Austen. They did encounter two small groups of Japanese soldiers and they scared them off, which confirmed their suspicions that the number of Japanese troops on the island was low. On September 24th, 1942 they started climbing the mountain and engaged in a battle with sixteen Japanese soldiers. Both sides were surprised, and the noise of the battle signaled the nearby Japanese troops that someone was attacking them. Maizuru Battalion charged Puller's men and managed to kill a total of thirty Marines while they suffered fewer casualties.

Puller had many wounded soldiers and they were simply in a trap. He called in for the reinforcement and the 2nd Battalion, 5th Marine Regiment arrived the next day. Puller ordered the wounded soldiers to remain in the protected area while he attempted to break free with the help of Lieutenant Colonel David McDougal and his men. They arrived at a bridge over the Matanikau River on September 26th, 1942 but were deflected by the Japanese soldiers who were guarding the crossing. There was no way to cross the river there so they tried to find another location. However, the Japanese sensed what they were planning and followed the troops wherever they went, attacking them as they got near the water. Griffith's Raider battalion joined the fight, hoping they would make a difference, and they came up with a strategy that could actually work. The Marines attacked the Japanese troops on September 27th and it was clear nothing was going their way. The plan was to make a diversion in order for Puller's men to surprise the enemy. But the Japanese were stronger, leading to a complete failure of the mission.

Seeing that the fight was going in the wrong direction, Chesty Puller ran directly to the shore and started signaling the nearby USS Ballard. He asked that they help him get all the men out because they were in a trap and couldn't move forward. USS Ballard fired at the Japanese troops while a landing craft arrived at the shore and rescued the surrounded Marines. In the end, the Japanese had fewer casualties and they eventually won the battle. The US Marines started fighting among themselves, especially the commanders who were in charge of the operation. They didn't have enough information which led to the defeat. Luckily, that was the only operation in Guadalcanal that had a bad outcome. Puller did save a lot of lives which had lessened the severity of the defeat, and his men thanked him for that. He received the Bronze Star Medal with Combat "V" for this mission.

Chesty Puller remained stationed on Guadalcanal and the next big mission for him and his men came in October of 1942. He was in command of 1st Battalion 7th Marines, and they were one of two units who were in charge of protecting the US airfield from the Japanese troops who made a tremendous progression over the non-occupied territory of the island. The Japanese soldiers had strength in numbers and felt confident they could take over the Henderson Field. Besides 1st Battalion 7th Marines, the 3rd Battalion of the US Army's 164th Infantry Regiment was at the location as well. They were attacked in the night between October 24th and 25th. The Japanese were hoping they would surprise the US Army but they returned the shots immediately. The gunfire lasted for hours and in the end, the US Army won and managed to protect the airfield. The US troops had 70 dead soldiers while the Japanese had a total of 1,400 casualties. Puller's Marines were clearly outnumbered, but they held their place in the Battle for Henderson Field and came out victorious. It was a heroic victory for the United States. Chesty Puller was regarded as a hero and received his third Navy Cross for that battle. Two of his Marines got Medals of Honor as well. But unfortunately, a couple of weeks later, Puller himself was shot on Guadalcanal. The good thing was that he was alive and suffered only minor injuries.

After a brief recovery, Chesty Puller was ready to get back to the front lines. He was in charge of the 7th Marine Regiment now, and they were deployed to New Britain, Territory of New Guinea. The war in the Pacific was raging and the Japanese had invaded numerous islands and territories, trying to remain dominant in that part of the world. Even though the United States had a stronger army, the Japanese were determined to win. The 7th Marine Regiment under the command of Chesty Puller was called to be a part in a mission which goal was to attack the Japanese 17th Division that was guarding the two airfields on New Britain. This encounter will be later called the Battle of Cape Gloucester. The battle began in December of 1943 and lasted until the middle of January of 1944. Chesty's 7th Marine Regiment was involved in heavy combat, but he showed true leadership while the 3rd Battalion, 7th Marines and 3rd Battalion, 5th Marines were under attack. Both the men and their commanders were left without the options for a brief moment but Chesty managed to put them back together. They were attacking the Japanese troops who were behind the heavy defense, protecting their positions with machine guns. After a long fight, the US Marines eventually found their way behind the enemy lines, securing the two airfields and defeating the enemy which was the main objective. Chesty Puller received his fourth Navy Cross during this mission which was already an important milestone in his military career.

He became a colonel on February 1st, 1944 and was made a commander of 1st Marine Regiment. Chesty and his Marine Regiment were sent to the battle of Peleliu which lasted throughout September and October of 1944. The US Marines suffered enormous losses during this encounter with the Japanese troops. The 1st Marine Regiment went into the battle with a total of 3,000 men, and lost 1,749 of them. Even though they were in a dire situation, Chesty refused to give up, constantly reorganizing his troops and sending them to attack the enemy regardless of the numbers. The commanding officer, seeing what was happening to Chesty and his men ordered for them to get out of there as soon as possible, saving the rest of the regiment. As the war was ending, Chesty Puller returned home to the United States in

November of 1944. He became the Director of the 8th Reserve District at New Orleans for some time, and would later move to Pearl Harbour to be in charge of the stationed Marines.

The Korean War

Even though Chesty Puller was getting older, he had a great reputation among the fellow Marines. After a brief period of peace, the United States became involved in the Korean War, and the troops were getting shipped out. He became a commander of the First Marine Regiment and was deployed to Korea in September of 1950 where he participated in the landing at Inchon. The objective was to take over Korea's capital Seoul, and the US Marines were successful. Chesty received the Silver Star Medal as well as a Legion of Merit. First Marine Regiment was involved in one of the most important battles of the Korean War - The Battle of Chosin Reservoir. It started at the end of November of 1950, meaning that the United Nations consisting of the United States, South Korea, and the United Kingdom had to face something even worse than the enemy himself. They were also battling an extremely cold winter which increased the number of casualties.

The United Nations suffered great losses, but they fought until the very end. Chesty's First Marine Regiment showed incredible bravery which led to him receiving the Distinguished Service Cross. The Battle of Chosion Reservoir was a failure for the United Nations but they learned a valuable lesson. The surviving troops evacuated from the territory of North Korea and remained stationed in the south. It is also important to mention that Chesty Puller told one of his most famous lines during this battle and the exact quote is: *"We've been looking for the enemy for some time now. We've finally found him. We're surrounded. That simplifies things."* Puller became a brigadier general in January of 1951 and he completed his duty. Then he returned to the United States in May of the same year. Not willing to retire yet, Chesty Puller went to California and was in charge of 3rd Marine Division. He became a major general in September of 1953.

The retirement and death

Chesty Puller remained involved in the Marines even after the Korean War, training the recruits. Unfortunately, he suffered a stroke in 1955 which meant that he simply had to retire. He was promoted to a lieutenant general in November of 1955. Wanting to enjoy his retirement but staying close to the Marines, he moved to Middlesex County, Saluda with his wife Virginia where they lived until their deaths. The Pullers had one son, Lewis Burwell Puller, Jr. and he wanted to follow in his father's steps. Fascinated by the tales and deeds of his heroic father, Lewis Jr. became a Marine lieutenant serving in the Vietnam War. Unfortunately, one wrong move led Lewis Jr. to a horrific injury. He stepped onto a mine which led to a loss of both of his legs. Unable to cope with his son's fate, Chesty started crying uncontrollably when he was Lewis Jr. in the hospital. Chesty Puller died on October 11th, 1971 and was buried in Middlesex County. His widow Virginia lived for two more decades.

The legend and the impact

Chesty Puller became a legendary figure in the Marine Corps. After all, he is still to this day the most decorated marine in the history. As a matter of fact, he was awarded five Navy Crosses and one U.S. Army Distinguished Service Cross for his service. Every Marine out there respects Chesty Puller and uses him as an inspiration. He has so many memorable quotes but one of the most frequently used is: *"Hit hard, hit fast, hit often."* It was his advice when asked how to win in a battle. His persona still has a large impact on the Marines of today because Chesty was a known disciplinarian who valued hard work. The

Marines who are training would often do an extra push-up for Chesty and would refer to him at least once every day.

His accomplishments on the battlefields are often told in boot camps or among the fellow Marines because the man created a myth around himself. Even the Marine Corps' mascot is always referred to as Chesty Pullerton. Lewis Burwell Puller Jr. who was devastated after his terrible injury in the Vietnam War made a name for himself as a writer and won a Pulitzer Prize for a book called *Fortunate Son: The Healing of a Vietnam Vet*. In this autobiographical work, Puller Jr. described how it felt to grow up in a family with such a famous military legacy and why his experience in Vietnam made him change his mind about the army and conflicts.

ROBERT HOWARD :
AMERICAN SOLDIER

"He was a gardener, a gentle man with massive hands and a velvet voice who worked on his roses and never once spoke of what he did in the war." - Melissa Gentch, daughter of Colonel Robert L. Howard

Robert Howard may be the most highly decorated American soldier since World War II.

He was born July 11, 1939, in Opelika, AL. His father and four uncles were paratroopers in World War II. Two of them died in combat and the other three died of wounds sustained after the war.

Howard had been forced to work early, having to support his mother and maternal grandparents. Both he and his sister picked cotton in their small town in Alabama.

"I remember when I was about seven years old," Howard said. "My dad was drafted and my mother had to go to work because back in those days the Army didn't take care of dependents like they do today. I had two brothers and two sisters. And my mother I think she got something like $45 dollars a month to provide for four children. My father was given six weeks of basic training and he was sent to Europe, and we didn't see him again for four years, six months, and about fourteen days, and he was drafted for one year. In fact, he didn't write home very often either, because the mail system wasn't as good as we have today in this country. So when I went to Vietnam the first time I use to think about how my dad didn't have a one year rotation, he went over there for 4 years, 6 months, and some 14 days and when he got home . He stayed drunk for two years. My mother solved that problem as she just divorced him."

Howard moved to Texas after the divorce and despite the rift between his parents he remained fond of his father and proud of his World War II involvement.

"Howard grew up in Southern gentility," military historian Vance Garrison said. "You opened doors for women, you went to church and you didn't use foul language. Everyone close to Howard knew that he detested vulgarity. He stood for honor and valor. He came from a place and era where your word was your bond and your character was your action. It should be emphasized also that he was a religious man born into a Christian family. Spiritual beliefs were rooted in the Alabama culture that he grew up in. He believed in the afterlife and wasn't afraid to die. It is this belief system that propelled and allowed him to do things that perhaps men who didn't have faith or less faith wouldn't do."

Howard joined the Army in 1956 at the age of seventeen and was assigned to the 101st Airborne Division. In 1965, during his first tour of duty in Vietnam, he was wounded by a bullet that ricocheted and sliced across his forehead. While recovering in a hospital, he was recruited by a Special Forces soldier to join the Green Berets.

By the age of thirty, he became a sergeant first class and arguably the most physically fit man in the army.

"Howard was a strong, strapping young man," Garrison said. "He was built like a lumberjack and looked like something you would see out of a Hollywood Casting office if they were casting for a man who looked the part of the heroic soldier. It is no surprise that he would later see some minor roles in movies, specifically cast as an instructor in John Wayne's *The Green Berets*."

He worked his way through the ranks, eventually becoming a staff sergeant at the highly classified Military Assistance Command, Vietnam – Studies and Observations Group (MACV-SOG). This was a 60-man Recon company, a top secret Green Beret team that completed classified missions behind enemy lines. As a member of the SOG (Studies and Observations Group) he did recon, invaded, attacked and disrupted the Vietnamese Ho Chi Minh trail network in Laos and Cambodia.

"If you were in SOG and you were willing to die," Howard said, "you wanted to have someone there with you that you didn't mind dying for, or with. It was knowing that we were making a difference in reducing American casualties and impacting the North Vietnamese and the VC that was part of what kept me there."

"The work Howard did with the SOG was highly classified," Garrison said. "So it can be argued that he performed a lot of heroics that we won't and never will find out about. They had different code names for everything. The Laotian cross-border efforts were called Daniel Boone and then renamed to Prairie Fire which Howard was a part of. He undoubtedly had to do things wherein there would be no witnesses present. Without any witnesses, there is no commendations or medals. But Howard was a humble man and realized that the missions trumped the medals."

LEGENDARY STUFF

Howard's heroics quickly became the stuff that Hollywood could only dream about.

There was an instance where he was in the food line at an American base and two NVA sympathizers on a motorbike tossed a hand grenade at the soldiers. While others dived for cover, Howard had other ideas.

He grabbed the M-16 out of the hands of a scared-stiff security guard, dropped to one knee and reeled off one shot on the Vietnamese attackers. The driver of the bike went down. The passenger got up and ran.

Howard chased the bomber for over a half-mile before killing him as well.

"What is striking about learning about Howard's heroics is his ability to make decisions instantly," Garrison said. "Some men would freeze or take cover. Howard would always take immediate actions, he didn't stand there mulling over possibilities. His knee jerk response was always to take action."

"In the military, in my case, you got a job to do," Howard recalled. "Its a level of responsibility. The same way on the battlefield, you got a split second to make a decision. And you have to make that decision based on training, based on the information of the current situation and you can't procrastinate."

THE RESCUER

Another instance of his bravery was when he and his recon team were laying beside an enemy highway in Laos. A Vietnamese convoy drove past. Howard ran alongside the enemy truck and threw a claymore mine at the enemy soldiers stuffed in the back, blowing them up.

Howard was always prepared for the unexpected. On one occasion he was riding in a Huey with Larry White and Robert Clough into Laos. They then unknowingly landed next to two heavily camouflaged enemy helicopters.

Their Huey was hit by gunfire immediately. White was shot three times and fell to the ground. Howard and Clough fired back.

Somehow, someway, their Huey lifted up out of the precarious situation and flew back into South Vietnam.

"Just knowing Bob Howard was ready to come and get you meant a lot to us," recon team member Lloyd O'Daniels recalled.

This would be the case of Joe Walker.

Walker had been on a recon team that had been overwhelmed near a Laotian highway. He was grievously injured and hiding with a Montagnard soldier, unable to move.

Howard got into position with twelve men and waited for darkness to arrive.

Then cloaked by the night sky, Howard moved in, feeling among bodies for heartbeats.

He eventually found Walker, feeling his signature horn-rimmed glasses on his face.

"You sweet son of a gun," Walker said as Howard dragged him to safety.

"Loyalty to the unit, mission and each other were essential elements on the RT (recon team)," Howard would say later. "The mission was always first, cowardice was not accepted, if it was observed through the course of a mission, it was handled honestly, with those concerned, and without prejudice We also knew that death and injury was anticipated, heck, almost expected...capture was not an option...we were truly dependent upon one other for individual and collective survival."

WHO WERE THE MONTAGNARDS?

The Montagnards were indigenous mountain people and seen as allies to stop Viet Cong advancement into the region. Howard was part of the special forces group that helped train these men in unconventional warfare.

These Montagnards were recruited and approximately 40,000 fought alongside American soldiers, allying themselves in the U.S effort to rid the region of the Viet Cong.

"They were quiet people," Garrison said, "But very determined. They also had skills in tracking as well as knowing the region very well. They were an asset to our efforts in Vietnam."

"They were mostly Chinese people. They came from tribes of the Hmong, Bru, Nung, Sedang and each came with their own identity and culture. They were fed up with Vietnamese persecution, losing thousands of loved ones who were killed or pushed out of their own lands. They were incredibly loyal to the Americans. Surely Howard found a lot of kindred spirits among them as they fought beside him."

MEDAL OF HONOR NOMINATIONS

Howard was recommended for the Medal of Honor on three different occasions for three specific actions during thirteen months between 1967-1968. The first two nominations were downgraded to a Silver Star and the Distinguished Service Cross due to the classified nature of the jobs in which Howard had been engaged.

The first of these missions occurred while Howard led a covert SOG platoon-sized mission in southeastern Laos on November 16, 1967.

While the majority of the troops were occupied with taking out an enemy cache, Howard's unit came upon four NVA soldiers who were promptly killed. His unit was then trapped by heavy machine gun fire in retaliation.

Howard then took it upon himself to take down the NVA's lead sniper and then charged the machine gun position, killing all of those inside.

Another machine gun opened fire on him. He was "pinned down...with a blazing machine gun only six inches above his head," but he recouped, shooting and killing an entire NVA gun unit at point-blank range. Then he crawled forward and threw a hand grenade into their remaining machine gun position, taking out their gun.

The NVA soldiers quickly recovered, however, and took over the same gun. Howard remained in the open and fired on them with a light anti-tank weapon, taking out the gun again.

His unit was then rescued by helicopter.

Howard was recommended for the MOH for his heroism here but it would be downgraded to the Distinguished Service Cross.

"There were situations there that I had to make a decision, 'do, not do, do and do', most of the time I think I made the right decision."

Howard then led a FOB-2 Hatch Platoon into Laos. They spent four days in the area until they were ambushed by Vietnamese troops, aided by a Soviet-built PT-76 tank. Undeterred by the enemy gunfire, Howard crept forward and took out the Vietnamese tank with a rocket.

A medivac helicopter coming to aid his unit was shot down, however, and things looked grim for the already wounded Howard. But again, showing unbridled grit and determination, he charged ahead three hundred yards through NVA machine gun fire to assist the two pilots and injured door gunner to safety.

Howard was wounded during this charge, fourteen pieces of shrapnel had become lodged throughout his body but all that seemed to do was piss him off.

He charged again, killing two of the Vietnamese soldiers and taking a third as a prisoner.

NVA anti-aircraft fire prevented the extraction of the platoon until the following day. Howard, his body riddled with shrapnel, leapt into action again as he took out the anti-aircraft gunner.

For a second time, Howard was nominated for a Medal of Honor for his actions but this was downgraded to a Distinguished Service Cross.

A month later, Howard served as a member of forty man Bright Light rescue mission into Cambodia. The team was in search of MACSOG Private First Class Robert Scherdin who had been missing from his recon team.

"Scherdin was on a mission with the SOG," Garrison said. "He was the assistant team leader and on a ten man recon team that had been dropped into Cambodia. The team had been composed of two Americans and eight Montagnards. And we're talking tough terrain here, mountains and clusters of thick bamboo. This region was particularly known for being a NVA hotbed."

Scherdin led his team into the region as he suspected enemy forces nearby. The unit soon became under heavy gunfire from a concealed enemy position. One of the Montagnards, a soldier named Nguang, witnessed Scherdin fall to the ground. Nguang tried to help Scherdin up but the soldier only groaned in pain. The gunfire continued and Nguang was wounded. He then quickly rejoined the other three rear members of the team as they moved away from the ambush site.

"The five members of the front team were shooting it out with the NVA," Garrison said. "Then theyrelented and the squad leader called in to the helicopter above, requesting an immediate emergency extraction. The lead team was extracted along with the four Montagnard members of the rear element. Unfortunately, Scherdin had to be left behind."

The next day a search and rescue (SAR) Bright Light platoon-size team was sent into the area to search for Scherdin. The team was led by 1st Lieutenant James R Jerson with Howard as the assistant team leader. They were assisted by 38 indigenous team members who inserted to the area to search for the missing American as well.

"Trying to hide from well-trained trackers and hunter-killer teams was difficult to say the least," Howard said. "It got particularly tough when we couldn't effectively mask our insertions. We used some deception, but still,we were forced to adapt and move rapidly from our infil sites. Lots of times we got pounced on right after arriving and needed immediate extraction."

The team moved up the mountain where they believed Scherdin was wounded, both Jerson and Howard discussed the probability that the enemy was still present. Their gut instincts proved correct as a Chinese-made claymore mine detonated, seriously wounding several team members including Jerson and Howard, who were knocked unconscious.

A two company, 250-man attack was then launched on Howard and his squad.

"The blast must have blew me back," Howard said. "Blew me upside down and I was just crumpled up on the ground. And when I finally was in a state of coming to, I couldn't see. And blood running down my face and that was what was in my eyes, I couldn't see. And I guess I started, I guess I was praying out loud. 'God please!' And I'm thinking I want to see. And I'm able to focus my eyes and I'm able to see all this stuff now and my web gear is blown up off me. My weapon is blown all to hell and then I realize what in the world did I survive to blow that weapon up like that? I had an AR-16. And I smelled the most horrible smell and I'm trying to look around and I realize that there is an enemy using a flamethrower and the people that had been caught in the kill zone, he was burning them."

When Howard came to, he found his rifle destroyed and his hands injured. He smelled the stench of burning flesh as a North Vietnamese soldier was using a flamethrower to torch the bodies of the American and South Vietnamese dead.

Howard then threw a grenade in the direction of the NVA soldier.

"I always carried an M33 grenade on the left side," Howard recalled. "It was taped in place and my initial intent was to use it on the enemy and myself because I knew I would be blown up pretty soon and burned up. And so as he moved toward me he could see me wrassling trying to get that grenade out, and he got close to me and he's looking at me, and I'm looking at him and we acknowledged each other. I could tell by looking at him he was a well-trained North Vietnamese soldier. He had the determination and look of hate on his face. And he also had an evil look in his eye, like I'm gonna kill you, I mean I just felt that. And I had kind of a smirk and a little smile because I had a grenade and he knew I had a grenade, the humor in battle. And I'm saying to myself subconsciously, I gotcha. No matter how bad I'm blown up, I got you and you know it and that was kinda the expression between the two of us. And you know what this guy did? He stopped using the flame thrower. He started yelling commands and he had moved about ten or fifteen meters from me and I said 'I don't have to blow myself up or blew him up but I said I'm gonna blow him up.' But you know I didn't have the heart to blow that guy up. So when I threw the grenade it really wasn't to throw the grenade to hit him, but it was kinda throw the grenade at the other enemy that he had called out of position and they come running over."

"And then at that point in time I could hear the lieutenant screaming, and that's when I had to totally ignore the enemy situation and my wounds. He's (Jerson) quite a ways from me and I couldn't walk so I had to crawl over to him. And so as I start dragging him away, we get attacked by an enemy, a frontal attack again, three or four of the enemy, and one of the sergeants in the platoon, one of the squad leaders, was back down the hill a little ways and he saw what I was doing as I crawled to him, he started laying down a base of fire and killed those enemy soldiers that were attacking me. But in that process one of them fired a weapon and he riddled me across the center of my body and an ammo pouch just blew up the ammunition and actually picked me up off the ground and pulled me away from the lieutenant. Now, this is a split second that I didn't want to go back. But to even hesitate not to go back makes you feel so bad. You gotta do what's right. And it was right (going back to help Jerson). If I didn't do it, there was nobody else that would do it. Who else is gonna do it? You gotta make a decision, you know everybody else they were either dead or wounded or they were in a position trying to help me. I had to go back, you know, but I didn't want to go back because I was aware of the situation. I was wounded pretty bad. And I knew I was wounded pretty bad but at least if I died they could look and say that guy died the way he wanted to die because I went back."

"And I know the condition of the lieutenant. And I know that there is nobody else who is going to be able to get that lieutenant but me. And I didn't want to go back. But I did. And I went back and dragged him, dragged him back and the sergeant was laying down a base of fire. And they got me in a position where I could command and give the commands and make decisions on the use of fire power. Make assessments on the medics that were treating the wounded and making sure that all our dead were accounted for. We had dragged them out of the kill zone and we had as many as we could whether were able to get down and establish defensive position and hold out for about sixteen hours until we could get some relief in there and evacuate."

With mangled fingers, he dragged the lieutenant back toward his remaining troops. The North Vietnamese soldiers began firing on Howard, shooting him in the foot.

Clutching a pistol given to him by a fellow soldier, Sergeant Howard shot several North Vietnamese soldiers and got the lieutenant down to a ravine.

"We had no choice but to stay motivated as leaders," Howard recalled. "As for our soldiers, we reminded them that God and country came before our needs."

Howard crawled from position to position, resupplying his men with ammunition and directing fire toward the encroaching enemy while requesting fire support.

A three and a half hour gunfight ensued and Howard saw it as their last stand.

"Here I come face-to-face with a platoon of enemy soldiers and so I'm standing with my weapon like this, and they fire directly at me and I fell backwards like this, and I didn't get killed," Howard explained.

The fight ended when, out of ammunition, he called in a 2,000-pound bomb.

"I said 'I want you to put it right on our position,'" Howard said. "It blew us and the enemy up. Next thing I know, we're still alive."

The unit was rescued as an emergency night evacuation was successful.

Howard was the last man to board the copter despite his many injuries, making sure that none of his men were left behind.

"I had one choice," Howard said, explaining his actions. "To lay and wait, or keep fighting for my men. If I waited, I gambled that things would get better while I did nothing. If I kept fighting, no matter how painful, I could stack the odds that recovery for my men and a safe exodus were achievable."

Jerson would later die of his wounds.

Undaunted, the rear element of the original team was reinserted into the battle site to search for Scherdin. The team had been comprised entirely of Montagnards and remained in the area for four days. It is unknown if they discovered the body of Scherdin as they died in a helicopter crash after their own emergency extraction.

Robert Scherdin was reported as Missing in Action.

"This is a very cliched thing for me to say but if the Vietnamese had a desire to account for our missing in action, they would," Garrison said. "Scherdin was one of thousands that have been unaccounted for by our government. If he survived those wounds, he was most likely captured then executed."

"There were numerous clandestine operations that were successfu. But you don't hear about them. You just hear about the ones that were detected and stopped. Make no mistake, Howard's teams had a well earned reputation as being one of the most effective deep-penetration forces in military history."

FIVE YEARS OF WAR

Howard would serve 58 months in Vietnam, spending the rest of his life picking out shrapnel from his body.

"I guess it's because I want to help in any way I can," Howard said explaining the long tenure of duty. "I may as well be here where I can use my training; and besides, I have to do it-it's the way I feel about my job."

With his actions during the attempted Scherdin rescue, he received the Medal of Honor from President Richard M. Nixon on March 2, 1971. True to form, however, Howard was informed of this as he was in the heat of battle.

"As I jumped into the mortar pit and jumped over the sandbags, I got hit in the foot and about that time one of the captains that had been in tactical operations had run me down with a three 2-F telephone and said 'I got the Chief of Staff of the army on the telephone. He's calling all the way from Washington, DC.' And I thought the Chief of Staff of the Army was calling to get an update on the enemy situation in which we're under attack right now from me on the battlefield. I'm a captain in charge of 218 Americans. Really, I thought they were kidding me when they said General Westmoreland. And he said 'Bob! How you doin?' I said 'Sir, the situation is pretty damn bad here. I said you want my honest opinion its pretty bad right now plus my foot hurts I just got shot in it!; And he said well, 'Congratulations! We gonna award you the medal of honor.' And I said 'Sir, I really appreciate that honor but I said I think I'm gonna have a problem getting out of here. He said 'No you won't.' And General Abrams, our lead commander did send his aircraft down and the airfield was still under attack. And they got me as close as they could to the plane and with the lieutenant colonel and we kinda struggled together and they were shooting at us and we got on the plane. We took about four hits on the takeoff."

The Medal of Honor citation credited him for his "complete devotion to the welfare of his men at the risk of his life."

RECEIVING THE MEDAL OF HONOR

"I didn't appreciate the honor itself until the award ceremony in Washington, DC and the courtesy that was extended to me by President Nixon and the first lady Mrs. Nixon. That's when I felt the responsibility and honor in receiving the award and the real responsibility that went with receiving the award."

President Richard Nixon placed the Medal of Honor around Howard's neck as family, friends and other dignitaries looked on.

"President Nixon put it around my neck and I turned real pale," Howard recalled. "And I thought I was brave and all that stuff, and when he put wreaths around me and around my neck and he said 'Bob, are you okay? You're mighty pale.' I almost fainted. I said 'I'm fine, sir, thank you so much.' And he said 'what are you going to do here in Washington today?' I said, 'I really appreciate being here, Sir and I think I'm going over to the Tomb of the Unknown Soldier immediately following this ceremony because I had my Dad and three of my uncles that were killed in World War II."

ANTI-WAR SENTIMENTS

"It was a very simple war and I'm a very simple man," Howard said, recalling the political climate of the times. "But I'm an American and I believe what we done in Vietnam was right. And we had a president of this country that was not too popular but he said, 'Before freedom is threatened Americans are challenged'. And I felt the challenge in Vietnam and I'm very proud of my service and I hope that I get to serve again some place somewhere in the fight for freedom for my country again someday."

"One of the unfortunate things about Howard," Garrison said, "is that he never got the just due from the broader public the way an Audie Murphy or Alvin York did. Or even today with the movie made about Chris Kyle. Americans in the 1970s did not want Vietnam and the anti-war sentiments prevented a lot of these brave men from receiving an overdue thank you. And yes, I know this is a cliché but it bares repeating because Howard was such a special soldier. And I don't think Howard was bitter about a lack of fanfare at all, that obviously doesn't fit in with his character. He was a humble and honorable man who saw himself as doing his duty. But as a student of history, you look at a sacrifice a guy has made and you don't want to see it ignored."

"You know, I had a job to do and that's leadership," Howard explained. "And I had a bad enemy situation. And the witnesses thought I went above and beyond what was required of my duty position. In other words, if I had not had done what I had to do, well then no one would have criticized me because I was blown up and laying on the ground but I still had the ability to reconstitute myself and overcome the enemy situation at a point in time to where I was successful in saving people's lives and pulling my platoon leader out of an ambush site that was being attacked by an enemy that had ambushed us. There is no doubt in my mind that there is many that I left on the battlefield that deserved the medal of honor but they died and didn't have witness statements that I was fortunate enough to have to be nominated by my fellow peers and my subordinates to receive the Medal of Honor."

LEAVING THE BATTLEFIELD

Howard left combat and became the training officer at the Army's Airborne School. After that he became a company commander in the 2nd Ranger Battalion at Ft. Lewis, Washington

Embracing his new role as a teacher, he became the officer-in-charge of Special Forces training at Camp Mackall in North Carolina and then the Mountain Ranger Training Camp at Dahlonega, Georgia.

"I teach them how to survive on the battlefield," he said. "I teach them how to weigh courage and fear. You can balance that."

He would lead marathon runs and long-distance rucksack marches, inspiring the younger soldiers by outworking them.

Howard would also go back to school. He received a bachelor's degree in police administration from Texas Christian University in 1973 and received two master's degrees from Central Michigan University, one in management in 1980 and the other in public administration in 1981.

He would then rise to commander of the Special Forces Detachment, Korea. The conjecture is that he could have gone higher in the ranks but he stirred about controversy by going public with the fact that he thought American POWs were still in Vietnam.

"I don't regret one day of my service," Howard said. "I could almost tell you the names of every man right now that made a sacrifice for me to be here today in the battles I was in."

"I was privileged to be born American. I was privileged to be born in the greatest nation in the world. God Bless you and your service. Never surrender your weapon and face the enemy."

He would retire as a full colonel and spend the next twenty years with the Department of Veterans Affairs as a liaison to other veterans.

In 2009, however, he would be diagnosed with terminal pancreatic cancer and was only given a few weeks to live.

He would day two days before Christmas on December 23rd, 2009. Survivors include two daughters from his first marriage, Melissa Gentsch of Waco and Denicia Howard of Fort Lauderdale, Fla.; two children from his second marriage, Army Sgt. Robert L. Howard Jr. of Fort Bragg, N.C., and Roslyn Howard of Hawaii; and four grandchildren.

'Take a man and make him a Soldier
   and put him thousands of miles away from home,
   empty his heart of all but blood,
   make him live in rain, sweat, and mud,
   this is the life he has to live,
   his soul to God he's willing to give,
   you peace boy's smoke your pipe
   and prance your style, but over here its worth our while,
   we have a lot of smoke, our style is freedom all.
   You burn your draft cards, march at dawn,
   and check your songs on the White House lawn,
   you all want to ban the bomb,
   the real enemy in war is in Vietnam,
   but your war is at home, you use your drugs
   and have your fun, then you refuse to use the gun,
   there's nothing else for you to do,
   My God help us in our prayers
   for our fellow Americans that are willing to fight
   for what seems to be right.
   He has seen an arm of a friend a bloody shred,
   he has heard so many times, this one here is dead,
   drag him out of the sun. O my God they took his gun.

I've heard that hundreds of times,
ladies and gentlemen that one statement.
It's a large price to pay, not to live another day,
but he had the guts to fight and die.
He paid the price for what did he buy?
He bought your life an unusual way
by his unselfish devotion to duty.
He died for freedom and the American way.
Keep his memory and pride
and please God help those Americans who can't decide.' - Robert L
Howard

ROCKY VERSACE AMERICAN SOLDIER

32

CARL BIANCHI

Humbert Roque "Rocky" Versace was born in Honolulu, Hawaii on July 2nd, 1937. Rocky's father was Humbert Joseph Versace, a Colonel in the Army who served over thirty years, moving the family from station to station while he served.

Rocky's mother was Marie Teresa Rios, a novelist who wrote under the name of Tere Rios. Her works included the Fifteenth Pelican on which the TV series The Flying Nun with Sally Field was based. An accomplished woman, she also worked as a photojournalist, reporter and editor for several military newspapers. She had been born in Brooklyn, New York and was of both Puerto Rican and Italian heritage. A devout Catholic, she took to writing early on. She would meet and marry Humbert, an accomplished man himself who had graduated in 1933 from the United States Academy West Point. Rocky would be the first of five children born from this union which includes Richard "Dick" Versace, the former coach of the NBA 's Indiana Pacers who was born three years after him.

"We had a pretty typical Italian-American family," Dick Versace recalled. "There's a lot of love. There's a lot of laughter. There's a lot of good food. And it always ends up in a fight."

BORN STUBBORN

When he was twelve years old, Rocky took the Catholic no-meat-on Fridays rule a step too far when he refused to eat jello, as he believed jello was made from calf hooves. He and his mother argued until she called in a priest to mediate their disagreement.

Rocky spent part of his teen years in Alexandria, Virginia, attending Gonzaga College High School for two years. In his junior year, he went to Frankfurt American High School in Germany before returning to the States and graduating from Norfolk Catholic High School.

"Rocky and I happened to be on the same bus," Michael Heisley, owner of the Memphis Grizzlies said. "Going to the same grade and we formed a bond. Over a period of time we became very, very close."

"I don't believe there was anything Mike wouldn't do for Rock," Steve Versace said. "And I don't think there is anything Rocky wouldn't do for Mike. You couldn't find two closer friends, I don't think."

He had gotten straight A's during his high school years with the exception of a space marked "deportment" wherein the nuns consistently gave him D's.

"He just wouldn't shut his big mouth," his mother said in a newspaper article. "He was bullheaded."

With his father away for military service, he would serve as the 'man of the house' over his two younger brothers.

"Going from school to school could not have been easy for Rocky," military historian Alan White said. "No matter how tough a kid is he knows that the friends he is making one year won't be around the next because of his father's occupation. So Rocky had to develop charisma, always being the new kid in school. He had a self-effacing persona that instantly put people at ease. Nobody ever had anything bad to say about Rocky another than the fact that he could be one stubborn sonuvagun."

WEST POINT OR PRIESTHOOD?

Rocky fluctuated between joining the priesthood after high school or following in his father's footsteps by entering West Point and joining the army. His father was a career military man as well as a West Point grad. After much deliberation, he would choose the military as his mother said that her son's "fierce and demanding" love of country and a charismatic demeanor would allow him to be a true leader of men.

His West Point classmates would later recall Rocky as "good-natured." He hunkered down and "plugged away", not allowing anything to deter from his path of becoming an officer. One classmate described him as someone who "bulled his way through" every obstacle the Army put in front of him.

Rocky became a champion wrestler and boxer at West Point, winning the Brigade Open Wrestling championship. During this time, he developed extraordinary physical strength, speed and endurance that put him in another level beyond his peers.

"Rocky was tall and lean with piercing eyes," White said. "He looked to be straight out of a Hollywood Casting office when looking for a young military man. But he had an open smile, engaging and warm, you would almost think he would be too nice to be a killer soldier."

He was described by nearly everyone who knew him as someone who fully took the motto "Duty, Honor, Country" to heart. Buttressed by a Catholic faith passed down to him from his family, Rocky would stand firm in his beliefs.

"He had a focus that put him a class above the majority of his peers," White said. "Whatever he did, he excelled at. He could have became a boxer, wrestler, marksman or Catholic priest. Whatever his chosen field would turn out to be, Rocky would have focused and excelled."

Versace graduated from West Point in 1959 and from there went to Ranger school. He earned his Ranger Tab on December 18th, 1959 after which he became a member of the Ranger Class 4-60. From there, Rocky would go to Airborne School and earn his parachutist badge.

FIRST TOUR OF DUTY

Rocky was sent to the Republic of Korea and served with the 3rd Battalion, 40th armor, 1st Cavalry Division. He was an M-48 tank platoon leader from March 1960 to April 1961. After this tour of service he was assigned to the 3rd U.S. Infantry (Old Guard) where he would once again be the tank platoon leader.

Rocky became involved in an orphanage while working in Korea and developed a soft spot for the children there. When he journeyed to Vietnam, he would spend the majority of his down time at an orphanage in the Mekong Delta.

Rocky then attended the Military Assistance Institute, took an Intelligence course at Fort Holabird, Maryland and the USACS

Vietnamese language course at the Presidio of Monterey. With the ability to speak both French and Vietnamese, Rocky would be well-prepared to be an asset in the Vietnam War.

"His tour of duties in the military," Heisley said. "Were really of 'service.' Not just service to his country but service to mankind."

"True to his nature, Versace would seek to bridge the gap in communication during his tour," White. "He had done some forward thinking and research in deciding to learn Vietnamese. This would obviously come in handy in dealing with both allies and enemies alike."

He became an S-2 adviser to the Vietnamese district chief in Ca May.

"He was incredibly strong for his size," Marine Don Price said in remembering Versace. "He always carried a rosary and a pocket Bible."

Quiet and self-effacing, Versace nonetheless had a down to earth charm that extended not only to his fellow soldiers but to the people of Vietnam, particularly the children.

FRIENDS NOT ENEMIES

Rocky would disregard the dangers of driving in the Ca Mau district in a jeep armed only with a pistol in order to engage the local populace. He visited the district's orphanage, schools, midwife facility, medical clinic, Catholic church, and jail where the US forces held captured Viet Cong. He insisted that the prisoners be well treated.

Along the way, he befriended an elderly Vietnamese priest with whom he chatted with in French. He spoke Vietnamese to the native people, becoming popular with the children as his pockets were filled with hard candy. The children dubbed him "day uy candy", which meant Captain Candy in Vietnamese.

"He really fell in love with the Vietnamese people," Steve Versace said. "He really felt that they needed the kind of support that we were able to give them."

Versace saw the people of South Vietnam as innocent victims of the Communist regime. He would take trips through the village to minister and spread American goodwill. He helped built dispensaries, put up tin sheeting that replaced thatch roofs and arranged for tons of wheat to feed family pigs. He then lobbied public schools in the United States to send soccer balls which would then be used by the Vietnamese children.

During Christmas of 1962, Versace wrote this in a letter home. "I am convinced that your taxpayers' money is being put to a very worthy cause—that of freeing the Vietnamese people from an organized Communist threat aimed at the same nasty things all Communists want—at denying this country and its wonderful people a chance to better themselves."

LAST TOUR OF VIETNAM

Despite his good-natured persona, Rocky had a "subtle seriousness" as Price described. "He was definitely a man on a mission."

"His knew it was going to be his last tour," White said. "But Rocky planned to join the Maryknoll priesthood with the idea of returning to Vietnam to run the orphanage. He already been accepted at Maryknoll and just needed to complete his military obligations. He didn't want to leave Vietnam because of his work with the orphanage. Interestingly, he had his request to stay in Vietnam go all the way up the chain of command to General Westmoreland. The General gave him an exception to spend his last sixty days on active duty in Vietnam. Normally, they would ship you back home with only two months left."

With only two weeks of service remaining, Rocky continued to serve as a MAAG intelligence adviser to the South Vietnamese Army (ARVN) in the An Xuyen Province.

A ROUTINE MISSION

During a briefing, Rocky would discover that an enemy unit had moved into the town of Le Coeur, eight kilometers from Tan Phu where he was currently located.

He reasoned that if the enemies continued on unabated that they would launch attacks on Tan Phu. Versace met with the unit's commander, Captain Philip N. Arsenault to voice his concerns over the encroaching enemy soldiers.

The two decided that an assault on Le Coeur would be necessary and they would deploy the troops in the following morning.

Their plan would be to send out three companies of CIDG and the local South Vietnamese soldiers. These Third Company would be under command of Vietnamese LLDB Lieutenant Lam Quang Tinh. These units would hit the enemy command post and secure Le Coeur, while the other two companies would be the back up, between Le Coeur and the U Minh forest to cut down retreating Viet Cong members.

"I'm going too," Rocky said after the strategy was finalized.

"MAAG advisers aren't allowed to accompany a team on operations," Arsenault responded.

"Look, we are undertaking this operation because of information obtained in my meeting with the district chief," Versace said. "That makes this a joint operation with the militia, which makes it MY responsibility to be involved."

"Rocky would win out in that argument," White said. "He had a strong resolve and there would be no changing his mind despite the fact that most soldiers in his position would be prepping to go home. So he went along on the mission."

The Special Forces team organized was Lieutenant Nick Rowe, Sergeant First Class Daniel Pitzer (who had medic duty) and Versace. The three soldiers would join Lieutenant Tinh and Third Company in the mission to secure Le Coeur.

"Rocky was indeed obsessed with the idea of duty, honor, country," Retired Lieutenant General Howard G. Crowell, Jr. said. "No one worked harder or more diligently than he.... He was so eager to accomplish his mission of gathering intelligence that it was bound to get him into danger sooner or later."

Nonetheless, the mission was considered routine as the amount of enemy soldiers involved looked to be small.

AMBUSHED

On the morning of October 29th, 1963, Rocky and the Special Forces team awoke early to set up the ambush. They left camp at 4:30 a.m. and an hour later the sun began to rise. By 6 o'clock, they had arrived at their predetermined location near a canal when the fire fight began.

"The Special Forces team initially thought they were dealing with a small band of Viet Cong moving in," White said. "They had no idea they were dealing with the tail end of a large snake."

"They thought they had a good plan. What few Viet Cong soldiers that were in that unit began running. But what Versace and the others didn't realize was that the retreating soldiers were leading them straight into an ambush."

The Vietcong retreated into a nearby village. Rocky and the team decided to go in deeper to search for the retreating enemy.

During the search, Rocky and the men came under fire. It became immediately apparent that that small unit they had first encountered was actually a part of a 600 man enemy unit. They were armed to he hilt and well-trained. The special force team was cut off from the other assisting units and pinned down by the enemy's superior firepower.

The three Special Forces men began covering for one another, one firing while the other reloaded. Rocky and the team fought back valiantly but were running out of bullets.

Rocky got hit in the back and legs, crumbling to the ground. Nick Rowe ran over to provide aid but the two were propelled forward after a grenade landed near them.

"Do tay len!" said a Vietnamese voice.

Rowe picked Rocky up and the two men were confronted by a pair of Vietcong soldiers with rifles pointed at them.

The assisting South Vietnamese unit had already been ambushed and killed which left the three Special Forces men alone. Rocky was captured with two other fellow soldiers, Lieutenant Nick Rowe and Sergeant Dan Pitzer.

There was another American unit only a few thousand miles away but they learned of the fight too late to help. The enemy's radio jammers had disrupted the main and alternate channels on all of the local military radios.

PRISONERS OF WAR

The captured men were then tied up, hands behind their backs, tied at their wrists and elbows which kept it impossible to keep their balance as they were pushed along the muddy paths. Rocky quickly realized that the enemy soldiers they had encountered were not the Viet Cong. They were the highly trained North Vietnamese soldiers.

The captured Americans were led down long and narrow paths in the jungle. They made temporary overnight stops in small huts and were thrown on a few canoe rides. Rocky had a fresh wound in his back as well as three bullet wounds to his leg. He hobbled along, his mind thinking of ways he would escape.

The men were separated. They were able to communicate on occasion but this was made difficult as they were kept far apart in separate bamboo cages. In formal compounds like those in Hanoi, the soldiers were able to use a TAP code to communicate. Here in the jungle, they had to devise different means of communication.

The men would use blood for ink, writing on small slips of paper or tree bark at pre-designated spots.

In a sly move, they would send messages by singing. The American prisoners would insert and exchange different words into the songs the guards may have heard but since the Viet Cong were not savvy in American colloquialisms they would be none the wiser.

SEPARATED FROM THE OTHERS

The enemy quickly separated Rocky from the others and kept him chained inside a tight six-feet by three-feet by two-feet bamboo cage which they kept elevated in a tree. This cage was infested with rodents.

During the hot Vietnamese nights, Rocky would be attacked by hordes of mosquitoes that quickly covered all of his exposed skin. The enemy fed him very little, he received no medical attention and had to endure interrogation sessions meant to extract phony confessions to deplete his morale.

He refused to cooperate and would be on the receiving end of beatings.

"The enemy used to parade him around," Brig. General Jack Nicholson said. "With rope around his neck. His hands tied."

A MOTHER'S HEARTBREAK

The news hit home of Rocky's capture and it devastated his family, particularly his mother. She had just secured a writing gig for the television series "The Flying Nun." Rios, however, was too distracted to work.

"Rocky's mother would later write to earn money to go to Vietnam," White said. "She wanted to travel to Vietnam and go from village to village to find her son."

TORTURE AND BRAINWASHING

The Viet Cong treated the three Americans as "war criminals" not as prisoners of war. They did this in defiance of the Geneva Convention and thus, treated their prisoners however way they saw fit.

Rocky tried to escape on several occasions. During one attempt, he had been caught while dragging himself through the mud on his injured leg. He had been trying to reach a canal where he believed he would be able to swim to freedom. It was a heroic attempt but with Rocky's weakened condition it did not have a high chance of success. He somehow managed to break free of the bamboo cage and crawled on his elbows, slowly through the mud with a cast iron ball attached to his leg.

And he still kept trying to escape.

Each time Rocky was recaptured, he was punished with decreased rations of food and an increase in the intensity of his torture.

"Versace had a fervent belief in God," White said. "He would often tell his captors that what was waiting for him after this life was far better than anything that they had planned."

The soldiers were also subject to constant brainwashing and propaganda speeches. These interrogation sessions were led by a man known as Mr. Ba.

Ba spent hours trying to brainwash the American soldiers, meticulously detailing how righteous the National Liberation Front (NLF) was in their efforts and how they had been misled during the 1954 Geneva Accords. Rocky would argue incessantly with his captors, refusing to give into their brainwashing techniques. He would repeat his name, rank, and date of birth whenever questioned.

"The Vietcong would use manipulative language as you would expect," White said. "They would try to convince the soldier that they were abandoned by their own country. That they were on the wrong side. They would withhold medical attention. They would withhold food. They wanted the soldiers to change to recant and express shame for their actions. They figured if they could do that, they would win. But they could not do that with Rocky. He refused to give in. He remained defiant."

The Vietcong made the soldiers repeat the same mantras over and over again, trying to convince them that the Communist way of life is better than that of the USA. They didn't realize the resolve and courage of the man they had in front of them, however.

They would try to twist his words around and he would give them a taste of their own medicine, insulting them in English, French and Vietnamese.

"You can make me come to this class," Rocky said during one interrogation session. "But I am an officer in the United States Army.

You can make me listen, and you can force me to sit here, but I don't believe a word of what you are saying, and frankly you can go to hell!"

"They were trying to break him and get him to say something," Dick Versace said. "That he did not believe in...you can just forget about it. Forget about it."

"Bravery is not physical toughness on its own," Heisley said. "Its mental and emotional commitment to your fellow human beings and to ideals."

On one occasion, Lieutenant Nick Rowe came upon Rocky as he washed his clothes in the river. True to form, he was arguing with his guard. Rowe called out to encourage Rocky and his fellow soldier responded with good cheer upon seeing his friend was still alive.

"Thank God, you're here Nick," Rocky said. "God bless you."

"Once, Rocky told our captors that...they might as well kill him then and there, " Rowe recalled. "If the price of his life was getting more from him than name, rank, and serial number. I'm satisfied that he would have it no other way. I know that he valued that one moment of honor more than he would have a lifetime of compromises."

"The defiance Rocky shown during this time was astonishing," White said. "Here he was being tortured, beaten and pretty much left for dead. He could have given in, if only to get a reprieve from the torture. But it would have been a fleeting thing and Rocky knew that. So he decided to go down fighting. It is heart breaking to read what he must have gone through but at the same time makes you marvel at one man's fighting spirit."

"Rocky walked his own path," Pitzer recalled. "All of us did, but for that guy, duty, honor , country was a way of life. He was the finest example of an officer I have known."

His refusal to be broken flummoxed Mr. Ba. Rocky was then declared to be a corrupt prisoner who would not be pardoned by the NLF. His escape attempts, they claimed, provided evidence that he was an incorrigible prisoner who would never show repentance for his "war criminal" actions.

"Rocky set an example as an American officer that the Viet Cong could not tolerate having known to the world" Rowe said.

GOD BLESS AMERICA

Rocky's time in captivity would last a total of twenty-three months.

"By spring of 1964 the farmers were talking about one U.S. prisoner in particular," Retired U.S. Army Brigadier General John W. Nicholson said. "They said he was treated very poorly, led through the area with a rope around his neck, hands tied, bare footed, head swollen and yellow in color (jaundice) and hair white."

"They stated that this prisoner not only resisted the Viet Cong attempts to get him to admit to war crimes and aggression, but would verbally counter their assertions convincingly and in a loud voice so the local villagers could hear."

"The local rice farmers were surprised at his strength of character and his unwavering commitment to God and the United States. The villagers' descriptions of Versace and his resistance became a topic of conversation we could count on hearing as we periodically operated in these remote areas."

"Villagers described Versace's deteriorating physical condition and added that the worse he appeared physically, the more he smiled and talked about God and America. Our interpreters told us that Captain Versace impressed the villagers with his faith and inner strength."

Nicholson would lead troops of South Vietnamese allies on missions to find POWs in 1963 and 1964. They would find freshly abandoned camps but no sign of the Special Forces men. They spoke to some villagers who told them about the Viet Cong troops parading an American from village to village.

"They did this to show the villagers the face of the enemy," White said. "Only it wound up backfiring. Versace looked sickly and starved. But remained dignified. He would defy his captors in their native language. They would then respond by hitting him in the face with the butt of their rifle. Then he would insult them again."

One woman recounted that she witnessed Versace being beaten then looking up to the sky with a smile,repeating Jesus' words "forgive them Father for they know not what they do."

"The Vietnamese people who witnessed this humiliation began seeing the American as a heroic martyr," White said. "So that is the likely reason his captors decided to kill him."

Finally fed up with his incorrigibility, the North Vietnamese decided to execute the soldier whose spirit they could not break. On September 26th, 1965, North Vietnam's "Liberation Radio" reported that Captain Humbert Roque Versace had been executed. "A payment of blood debts to the Vietnamese people," they announced.

The last time his fellow soldiers heard Rocky's voice, he was singing "God Bless America."

DEATH AND AFTERMATH

Rocky's body was never recovered.

His headstone at Arlington National Cemetery rests upon an empty grave.

When his parents learned of their son's fate, they made every effort to find out about what happened. His mother would go to Paris in the late 1960s and lobby to see the North Vietnamese delegation as their diplomats arrived for peace talks. Marie's efforts, however, would be unsuccessful.

His mother would go on to write about her sorrow in poems. One of her poems below, shows how his mother didn't know if she should write in the present or past tense.

"She did not know whether he was dead or alive," Stephen Versace said.

Missing In Action
*My son is * was*
*He often did * does*

*His eyes are * were brown*

"Not a day goes by," Rios Versace said in a newspaper article, "that I don't wonder about what my son would be doing had he survived. You think about every angle, every possibility. 'You say, 'What if...what if..what if?"

"But," she said, "there's conclusion."

Lieutenant Nick Rowe would remain in the camp for another three years until he overpowered a guard and escaped. Rowe would become the only POW during Viet to successfully escape captivity. He would appeal to President Nixon to award Versace for his actions both before and during their capture.

Rowe would later be killed in the Philippines in 1988 while he served as a military adviser.

Rocky was nominated for the Medal of Honor in 1969 but that proved to be unsuccessful as well. He was instead given the Silver Star mostly due to a "poorly written" account of his actions during his time of captivity.

His family and friends, however, didn't rest until Rocky got his Medal of Honor. In July of 2002, Rocky was posthumously awarded the Medal of Honor by President George W. Bush. This would mark the first time an Army POW had been given the Medal of Honor for his heroism in captivity.

"In his defiance and later his death," Bush said during Rocky's MOH ceremony. "he set an example of extraordinary dedication that changed the lives of his fellow soldiers who saw it firsthand. His story echoes across the years, reminding us of liberty's high price and of the noble passion that caused one good man to pay that price in full."

"One of Rocky's superiors said that the term 'gung-ho' fit him perfectly," he noted. "Others remember his strong sense of moral purpose and unbending belief in his principles. As his brother Steve once recalled, if he thought he was right, he was a pain in the neck. If he knew he was right, he was absolutely atrocious."

"Rocky was an extraordinary guy," Dick Versace said. "He was passionate. Fierce. The real Rocky was a compassionate, caring loving person who had ferocity of belief. He believed that what he was doing was altruistic that it was good. It was for the general good. He believed that."

"Fiercely."

\#

ROY BENAVIDEZ : AMERICAN SOLDIER

49

MICHAEL LOPEZ

"If the story of his heroism were a movie script, you would not believe it" –
Ronald Reagan on Roy Benavidez

Roy Benavidez was born on August 5, 1935 in Lindenau, Texas in DeWitt County. His father, Salvador Benavidez was a Mexican-American and his mother Teresa Perez was a Yaqui Indian. Salvador was described by his son as a "tall, graceful man" who loved to sing and dance. There was some family consternation when Salvador decided to marry Teresa as his mother was a Yaqui Indian. The Yaqui Indians at that time were considered a savage and primitive people who stayed to themselves. Neither family approved of the union but they went through with their marriage independent of anyone's blessing.

EARLY LIFE

Benavidez was born in his mother's bed with the help of a midwife. The family had a self-sufficient farm, raising chickens, a vegetable garden, and a milk cow. His parents, however, were still unfamiliar with the techniques of pasteurization and this led to the eventual illness of his father.

In 1937, the Benavidez family welcomed a new addition in Rogelio but Salvador died that same year. He had contracted tuberculosis from the milk cow. His father's sister, Isabel, came to assist with the care of Rogelio and Roy.

Roy's mother decided to move to a town called Cuero where she would find work as a domestic. A year after his father's death, she would marry a man named Pablo Chavez. This union would result in the birth of a sister named Lupe a year later. Roy was not particularly close to Pablo but stated that "my stepfather was not cruel to Rogelio and me, but neither did he pay us much attention."

Tragedy struck again for Benavidez at the age of seven his mother came down with tuberculosis. The doctor with whom she had worked as a housekeeper for did his best to try and save her but she eventually died at home. Benavidez recalled her funeral as a "simple one" and stated that she was "buried in a section reserved for people who couldn't afford a plot."

Roy saddened by the loss of his mother, also felt an immense amount of fright as he did not know where he would live. He worried that he and his brother Rogelio would be separated. His stepfather's family would ultimately take care of his sister Lupe. He had a seldom seen uncle named Nicholas, however, that arrived at his father's funeral. After the service, he informed the two boys that he would be taking care of them. His mother had arranged for this in the event of her death and the two boys went with their uncle to El Campo, Texas.

Benavidez learned valuable lessons at the feet of his Uncle Nicholas and grandfather Salvador. Both men would try to instill a sense of honor and morality in the headstrong young man but Roy remained rough around the edges. The boys were required to work at a young age, Roy would take to shining shoes at the local bus station as he already had experienced doing that in Cuero, as he would shine the shoes of the local cowboys. He would then give all of his earnings to his Aunt Alexandria who kept all of the earnings of the children (Roy would live with eight other cousins). Seeking an outlet for his anger, his family enrolled him in a local boxing program where he ascended to the Golden Gloves finals until finally being beaten. When approached by his conqueror in the locker room after a well-fought match, Benavidez grabbed him and shoved his face in the toilet.

Violent outbursts like these continued until the age of fifteen when Benavidez dropped out of high school. He continued working odd jobs, primarily pumping gas full time. He began keeping bad company, getting into trouble, and his Uncle Nicholas warned him of his choice of friends.

"Like a dummy I dropped out of school," Benavidez recalled. "I learned early in life 'why dig a ditch when you can supervise the diggin.' My adopted father would tell me that 'an education and a diploma is a key to success. Bad habits and bad company will ruin you.'"

Benavidez found full-time work changing tires at a local Firestone store, finding himself in the employ of a Christian man named Art Haddock. He enjoyed the work but soon realized that the job was a dead end one. He thought about the prospect of returning the school but nixed the idea as he did not want to be considerably older than the other students. He thought about taking the high school equivalency test and going to junior college but decided against that as well.

He joined the National Guard but still remained at the Firestone store. Seeing that he was on a road to nowhere, Haddock decided to have another sit-down talk with him.

"For a nineteen-year old kid, Raul, this is not a bad job. But is it going to be a good job for you when you're twenty-nine or thirty-nine?"

Roy saw the writing on the wall as the machines had taken over the jobs as field workers and his family was feeling the pinch. He knew that he needed education. The only alternative at the time was the army.

Deeming himself too old to return to school, Benavidez would join the Texas Army National Guard in 1952 or 1955 (the reported dates vary) as he "liked what he saw in the men in uniform."

He would meet his future wife during this time, Hilaria "Lala" Coy. He began to think of ways to get her attention as he thought her to be the "prettiest girl in town by far." She would arrive at local pick-up baseball games and Roy would try extra hard to do well but ultimately screw-up. The two eventually hit it off, however.

On June 7th, 1959, Benavidez married Lala in El Campo, Texas after he sent his uncle, grandfather and priest to ask Lala's father for his blessing.

MILITARY TRAINING

Benavidez would then be assigned to Military Police training at Fort Gordon, Georgia. Throughout his training, he would get into trouble because of his stubbornness and short fuse.

"The darn recruiters never told me what the training was like," Benavidez said. "For every mistake that you make, you do push-ups. I'm one of those guys that helped push Georgia into South Carolina doing push-ups."

That same year, he completed airborne training and was assigned to the 82nd Airborne Division at Fort Bragg, North Carolina. It was here during airborne training that all of the teachings of his Uncle Nicholas came to the forefront of his psyche. "Be the best, in whatever, you do, be the best," Benavidez recalled his uncle saying. "He meant that to extend to chopping cotton, pulling beets, shining shoes, or fixing tires. I was determined to be the best. Being in Airborne was my next step toward that goal, and I planned on being the best trooper they ever had go through that jump school."

"I heard about the extra pay that you get for jumping out of airplanes," Benavidez said. "I wanted to learn a skill. I wanted money in my pocket. I wanted good clothes. I wanted to have a car."

It was at Fort Bragg that he began training for the elite Army Special Forces, becoming a member of the 5th Special Forces Group and the Studies and Observations group (SOG).

"I heard about the Green Berets," Benavidez said. "We in the special forces are trained to go deep behind enemy lines with little or no support at all. We're trained in our specialties"

Benavidez received training in multiple disciplines in addition to weapons, he learned about oceanography, meteorology, and photography. He also crossed trained as a medic while becoming a trained linguist and interrogator.

In 1965, Roy was sent to South Vietnam as adviser to an ARVN infantry regiment. While out on patrol, he had the misfortune of stepping on a landmine.

"I stepped on a landmine (in Vietnam) and woke in in the Philippine Islands on Clark Air Force Base and was immediately sent back to the United States for treatment. Physicians at Fort Sam Houston informed him that he would never walk again."

Benavidez, however, would not accept their diagnosis. He grew angry at the media criticism of the US military involvement in Vietnam and used that rage to begin a training program in an attempt to walk again.

Rebelling against physician's orders, he would get out of bed, crawling on his elbows and chin to a wall near his bedside, prop himself against the wall and attempt to lift himself up. He started by wiggling his toes, then his feet and then after several months of this excruciating routine that often left him in tears, he was finally able to push himself up the wall his his ankles and legs.

"My back would be killing me," Benavidez recalled. "I begged God to please help me. I'd be crying. I'd get to the wall and I'd set myself against the wall. And I'd back myself up against the wall and I'd stand there. Like Elijah, the Indian. I'd stand there and move my toes. Right and left. Right and left. Every single chance I got, I wanted to walk. I wanted to go back to Vietnam."

"Because of what the media was saying. Our presence wasn't needed there, they burned the flag. I saw a lot of patients coming back. Limbs missing. And I wanted to go back. I was determined. I remember what I was taught in jump school. That old master sergeant would tell me 'Benavidez, 'quitters never win and winners never quit'. What are you?"

"I'm a winner."

Amazingly, Benavidez never gave up hope during this time despite the grim medical diagnosis.

"I remember in my special forces training," Benavidez recalled. "One of the training missions I was on, I remember that my leader would tell me 'faith, determination and positive attitude'. A positive attitude will carry you further than ability. You can do it, Benavidez. You can do it.' I never forgot those three words. Never. So there I was at night. I'd slip out of bed. The nurses would catch me sometimes. They would chew me out. Give me a sleeping pill. Put me to sleep. Then they would tell the doctors in the morning. I was determined to walk. Nine months later, here comes my medical discharge papers. And I told the doctor, 'Doctor, look what I can do.' He said 'Sergeant, I'm sorry. Even if you could stand up, you'll never be able to walk.' I jumped out of bed, I stood right before him, my back was aching, I was crying. And I moved just a little bit. And the doctor said 'Benavidez, 'if you walk out of this room I'll tear the papers up.'

"I walked out of that ward."

Benavidez had a limp but he made it out, going back to Fort Bragg, North Carolina where he began his own physical rehabilitation program. He walked everyday and built his endurance up to a five to ten mile run per day. He continued this workout routine until he once again became fit for combat.

"Doing fifty to a hundred push-ups a day," Benavidez said. "Then I made three parachute jumps in one day. I was ready to go back to Vietnam. Physically and mentally ready to go back. My orders were to go to Central America as an adviser but being a non-commissioned officer and knowing some of the good officers in the right places, my orders were diverted."

Benavidez was sent back to Vietnam in 1968. In April of that year, he and a friend were dropped behind enemy lines on an intelligence gathering mission. Two days later, his friend had been shot in his eye, back and legs. Their mission completed, Benavidez could not leave his friend behind.

He called for an extraction helicopter to come and get them out. The helicopter came and they dropped down one of the "McGuire Rigs", a cargo tie-down strap used to extract soldiers from areas with a less than ideal pick-up zone.

"The McGuire Rig is nothing but a piece of rope," Benavidez said. "Nylon and a hook. And in this case there were two ropes. We hooked on but the enemy was firing at us. We pulled up high into the canopy of the jungle, our rope started to twist and rub, and it burns when it rubs. And we cleared the canopy and our ropes were complete twisted and rubbing. And there was a non-commissioned officer riding in the helicopter."

Luckily, the officer saw the two ropes rubbing together and saw the threat in the ropes burning and tearing off. The officer immediately took action.

"He was riding safety and when he saw me and he saw those two ropes burning, he immediately tied himself with a rope around his waist and he pulled himself out of the helicopter and undid those two ropes, separating them. That's dedication, that's love of fellow man and country. I'll never forget that man."

The enemy continued to fire on them but Benavidez and his friend were extracted to safety. His friend was taken immediately to the hospital but didn't make it.

SIX HOURS IN HELL

A few days later, Benavidez was in a staging area, waiting for his next assignment when he would hear answer a call that would change his life forever.

"I heard something on the radio, something like a popcorn machine," Benavidez recalled. "Pop, pop, pop! Then I heard a voice 'Get us out of here! Get us out of here! Come and get us out quick asap! I asked the radio operator 'who are those men?' and he said 'I don't know.' And I saw some helicopter pilots running to the flat land. Scrambling, I ran right behind them."

"We saw a helicopter come in that had a door gunner slumped over his weapon. When the helicopter landed I unstrapped the door gunner, Michael Craig, nineteen years old. We just just celebrated his 19th birthday in March. I cradled him in my arms and his last words were 'my God, my mother and father.'"

"I asked the pilot who were the people on the ground he said 'Hey, that's the black NCO, that non-commissioned officer that saved your life the other day, remember? I said 'Leroy Wright'. Leroy always got picked for top secret assignments him and Musso and O'Connor. So it was an instant reaction. I saw a bag of medical supplies that I picked it up and I went over to my helicopter. Got on the helicopter,we got on the phone and the controller said 'You can't go in there, you can't go in. It's too hot.' Little did I know that I was going to spend six hours in hell."

Benavidez would soon discover that the distress call came from a twelve-man Special Forces patrol that included nine Montagnard (Vietnamese mountain soldiers) that were surrounded by an NVA infantry battalion of 1,000 enemy soldiers.

The following account, presented by Ronald Reagan during Benavidez' Medal of Honor ceremony, recounts what took place after Benavidez boarded that helicopter.

Master Sergeant (then Staff Sergeant) Roy P. BENAVIDEZ United States Army, distinguished himself by a series of daring and extremely valorous actions on 2 May 1968 while assigned to Detachment B56, 5th Special Forces Group (Airborne), 1st Special Forces, Republic of Vietnam.

On the morning of 2 May 1968, a 12-man Special Forces Reconnaissance Team was inserted by helicopters of the 240th Assault Helicopter Company in a dense jungle area west of Loc Ninh, Vietnam to gather intelligence information about confirmed large-scale enemy activity. This area was controlled and routinely patrolled by the North Vietnamese Army. After a short period of time on the ground, the team met heavy enemy resistance, and requested emergency extraction. Three helicopters attempted extraction, but were unable to land due to intense enemy small arms and anti-aircraft fire.

Sergeant BENAVIDEZ was at the Forward Operating Base in Loc Ninh monitoring the operation by radio when these helicopters, of the 240th Assault Helicopter Company, returned to off-load wounded crew members and to assess aircraft damage. Sergeant Benavidez voluntarily boarded a returning aircraft to assist in another extraction attempt. Realizing that all the team members were either dead or wounded and unable to move to the pickup zone, he directed the aircraft to a nearby clearing where he jumped from the hovering helicopter, and ran approximately 75 meters under withering small arms fire to the crippled team.

Prior to reaching the team's position he was wounded in his right leg, face, and head. Despite these painful injuries, he took charge, repositioning the team members and directing their fire to facilitate the landing of an extraction aircraft, and the loading of wounded and dead team members. He then threw smoke canisters to direct the aircraft to the team's position. Despite his severe wounds and under intense enemy fire, he carried and dragged half of the wounded team members to the awaiting aircraft. He then provided protective fire by running alongside the aircraft as it moved to pick up the remaining team members. As the enemy's fire intensified, he hurried to recover the body and classified documents on the dead team leader.

When he reached the leader's body, Sergeant BENAVIDEZ was severely wounded by small arms fire in the abdomen and grenade fragments in his back. At nearly the same moment, the aircraft pilot was mortally wounded, and his helicopter crashed. Although in extremely critical condition due to his multiple wounds, Sergeant Benavidez secured the classified documents and made his way back to the wreckage, where he aided the wounded out of the overturned aircraft, and gathered the stunned survivors into a defensive perimeter. Under increasing enemy automatic weapons and grenade fire, he moved around the perimeter distributing water and ammunition to his weary men, re-instilling in them a will to live and fight. Facing a buildup of enemy opposition with a beleaguered team, Sergeant BENAVIDEZ mustered his strength, began calling in tactical air strikes and directed the fire from supporting gunships to suppress the enemy's fire and so permit another extraction attempt.

He was wounded again in his thigh by small arms fire while administering first aid to a wounded team member just before another extraction helicopter was able to land. His indomitable spirit kept him going as he began to ferry his comrades to the craft. On his second trip with the wounded, he was clubbed from behind by an enemy soldier. In the ensuing hand-to-hand combat, he sustained additional wounds to his head and arms before killing his adversary.[5][1] [note 1][2] He then continued under devastating fire to carry the wounded to the helicopter. Upon reaching the aircraft, he spotted and killed two enemy soldiers who were rushing the craft from an angle that prevented the aircraft door gunner from firing upon them. With little strength remaining, he made one last trip to the perimeter to ensure that all classified material had been collected or destroyed, and to bring in the remaining wounded.

Only then, in extremely serious condition from numerous wounds and loss of blood, did he allow himself to be pulled into the extraction aircraft, Sergeant BENAVIDEZS' gallant choice to join voluntarily his comrades who were in critical straits, to expose himself constantly to withering enemy fire, and his refusal to be stopped despite numerous severe wounds,

---

1. *https://en.wikipedia.org/wiki/Roy_Benavidez%23cite_note-DAGO2501-5*

2. *https://en.wikipedia.org/wiki/Roy_Benavidez%23cite_note-6*

saved the lives of at least eight men. His fearless personal leadership, tenacious devotion to duty, and extremely valorous actions in the face of overwhelming odds were in keeping with the highest traditions of the military service, and reflect the utmost credit on him and the United States Army.

What wasn't recounted in the above detail is the amount of hand to hand combat that Benavidez endured as well as the fact that he was declared deceased. One of the dead soldiers was, in fact, Leroy Wright, the officer that saved Benavidez earlier that week by untwisting the ropes of the McGuire Rig. Wright had classified documents in his possession and Benavidez knew it was his duty to retrieve them. In order to do that, however, he would have to go through the aforementioned "Six Hours of Hell".

"I was hit in the mouth with the butt of a weapon," Benavidez recalled. "My jaws were locked. After my last return back to the helicopter when I was boarded on, I was holding my intestines in my hand, at least that's what they told me. We lifted up, the helicopter had over its payload. Bullets was flowing on both sides of the helicopter, we landed at Loc Ninh, our staging area. And started unloading, started identifying the bodies. They found I loaded three dead enemy soldiers in that helicopter. I didn't want to leave anybody behind. My mission was to recover any classified material so if any body had it he was on the helicopter. So they left the three enemy soldiers on the side 'cuz I sorta look Oriental and they thought I was one of them so let me lay right next to 'em. And they were putting us in body bags. And I remember my feet being lifted and I was being inserted into the boy bag and I could hear that zipper coming up and I was like 'Oh my God, no, my eyes were shut because I had blood all over my face, the blood had dried all up in my eyelids. And I couldn't talk because my jaws were locked and I could hear the zipper coming up and coming up and one of my buddies was doing the Mexican hat dance and he's like 'That's

Roy, that's Roy Benavidez and the doctor is like 'Sorry, there's nothing I could do for him.' And that zippers coming and there's nothing I could do, I'm covered in my own blood and finally later Gary Cunningham made that doctor at least feel my heart beat. When I felt that hand on my chest I made the luckiest shot I ever made in my life. I spit in the doctor's face. So the doctor said 'I think he'll make it.'

PRAYING TO GOD

During this time, Benavidez underwent both a spiritual and physical transformation. As he was evacuated back to safety, he held on to his friend and did his best to encourage him.

"I was cleaned up and put in a helicopter alongside my buddy. We got airborne and I said 'Hold on, buddy, just hold on. We gonna get some medical attention.' And his grip tightened up on me and then he let go. I said 'Oh God, why do you put me through this test? Why? You help me get these men out. Save 'em, save this material and now you take them away from me!'"

Benavidez was moving and thrashing about so much that the co-pilot thought he was gasping for air. The co-pilot then got out of his seat, took out his bayonet and looked ready to perform a tracheotomy on Benavidez.

"I was about to kick him out the helicopter!" Benavidez recalled. "That's just too much for one day! So we landed at hospital in Loc Vinh. I was wheeled to the operating room. And as I was being lifted to the operating room table, I saw this nurse crying, on her hands and knees yelling, asking God, 'Why do you do this to these men? Why?' She was just crying and I turned a little bit to my left I saw on the other operating table, a man that had both legs and both arms missing."

"I passed out. I woke up in a ward and one of my buddies was laying next to me. We were so bandaged up, we couldn't even talk. We managed to wiggle our toes to make sure we were still alive. After a short while my buddy was transferred from there and I thought he had died I was transferred to Japan. I remember this nurse kept yelling at me 'Benavidez, you're not gonna die on me! I'm gonna pinch you every time you close your eyes. I'm gonna pinch you, I'm gonna pinch you!'

Benavidez made it to Japan but the doctor was in shock at his physical condition.

"I remember the doctor saying 'what in the world happened to you?' I had blue spots, red spots all over me. I said 'that lady kept pinching me up there.'"

RECOVERY

Benavidez was then transferred back to Fort Sam Houston, the Beach Pavilion and he stayed in the hospital for almost a year. He then recovered enough to resume his military career before turning to public speaking.

Benavidez became a motivational speaker for schools, civic groups and anyone who needed his help.

"I wanted to help anyone that I could help," Benavidez said. "My life was spared for a reason. A lot of people call me a hero, I appreciate that title. But the real heroes are the ones that gave their live for this country. The real heroes are our wives and mothers above all, the heroes are the future leaders of our country, the students learning to say no to drugs."

"You know, there's a saying among us veterans, for those who have fought for it, life has a special flavor the protected will never know. You have never lived, 'till you almost died. And it is us veterans that pray for peace most of all. Especially the wounded, because we have to suffer the wounds of war."

One of the questions that hounded Benavidez throughout his retire is if he would do it all again.

"In my twenty-five years in the military I feel like I've been overpaid for the service to my country, Benavidez said. "There'll never be enough paper to print enough money nor enough gold in Fort Knox for me to have, to keep me from doing what I did. I'm proud to be an American and even prouder that I earned the privilege to wear the Green Beret. I live by the motto of duty, honor, country."

Benavidez received the Distinguished Service Cross for extraordinary heroism and four Purple Hearts. In 1969, he was assigned to Fort Riley, Kansas until he was transferred three years later to Fort Sam Houston, Texas. He remained at Fort Sam Houston until his retirement

In 1980, Brian O'Connor, the former radioman of Benavidez's Special Forces team in Vietnam, gave a stirring account of the battle that occurred on May 2nd, 1968. O'Connor himself had been severely wounded and he was evacuated to the united States before he could release a statement on Roy's heroics.

It would be O'Connor's report that would serve as the necessary eyewitness so that Roy's Distinguished Service Cross could be upgraded to Medal of Honor.

Fighting was not over for Benavidez, however, as he learned that the Social Security Administration planned to cut off the disability payments that he had been receiving since his retirement as well as the payments for thousands of other Vietnam vets. Shortly before Memorial Day 1983, he went to Capital Hill and argued with the House Select Committee on Aging to convinced them to abandon their plans. He still had two pieces of shrapnel in his heart, a punctured lung and remained in constant pain from his wounds.

Benavidez came before the House Select Committee wearing his Medal of Honor. He informed them that "the Administration that put this medal around my neck is curtailing my benefits.'

The government, however, believed that Benavidez could still find employment.

"It seems like they want to open up your wounds and pour a little salt in," Benavidez said. "I don't like to use my Medal of Honor for political purposes or personal gain, but if they can do this to me, what will they do to all the others?"

Amazingly, Benavidez received a lot of criticism for collecting disability payments. It took everything in his power to get out of bed in the morning, his war-time injuries cost him so much pain. Yet there were those who thought he should go out and work a nine-to-five like everyone else. The truth was, he couldn't. It took everything in his power just to get out of bed in the morning.

President Reagan became "personally concerned" about Benavidez' complaint and ten days later the the Secretary of Health and Human Services, Margaret M. Heckler, revealed that the disability reviews would become more "humane and compassionate.'"

In July of 1983, an administrative law judge ruled that he should continue receiving payments.

ILLNESS AND DEATH

Benavidez would have his right leg amputated in October of 1988. He would pass away on November 29, 1998 at the age of 63 at Brooke Army Medical Center. He suffered from respiratory failure and complications of diabetes.

His services were held at St. Robert Bellarmine Catholic church, the church where he had married, his three children had married and where he attended mass every Sunday. His body was returned to Fort Sam Houston's Main Chapel for a public viewing while his friend Archbishop Patrick Flores presided over his Catholic funeral mass at San Fernando Cathedral

He was then buried with full military honors at Fort Sam Houston National Cemetery.

Subsequently, several schools in Texas, a National Guard armory and an Army Reserve center were named for him.

CARLOS HATHCOCK : American Sniper

66

AMY PAULSEN

There are few names at the top of the list of military war heroes as well known or inspiring than Carlos Hathcock. His career, skills and tactics have had an enormous impact on military strategies across the armed services. A devoted Marine, he couldn't have known how much he would change the face of military strategy for not only his branch but the Army and Navy as well. A war hero, landmine survivor, multiple sclerosis sufferer, Sergeant Hathcock certainly had an impressive life. The stories of his escapades in the jungles of Vietnam precede the quiet and gentle man and serve as a startling contradiction. He was a sniper who didn't like killing, but he was damn good at it.

Famous Sniper and Marine, Carlos Norman Hathcock II, who was also known as White Feather, was born in Little Rock, Arkansas on May 20, 1942. The only child of Carlos and Agnes Hathcock, he grew up in in the sticks of Arkansas in their small house. But at a young age, Carlos went from living with his parents to staying with his grandmother after his parents separated. It is there where he would spend the rest of his childhood. While on a trip to visit some of his relatives in Mississippi, he picked up his first gun. A natural, he began shooting and hunting at an early age, and was motivated to get better at hunting in order to help feed his poor family. When he was asked about learning to hunt as a child, Carlos had this to say "As a young'n, I'd go sit in the woods and wait a spell, I'd just wait for the rabbits and the squirrels, 'cause sooner or later a squirrel would be in that very tree, or a rabbit would be coming by that very log. I just knew it. Don't know why, just did." He was a natural hunter and had already begun practicing the ability to become one with the environment. His target of choice were mostly the squirrels and rabbits he would find on those occasions. Often, he would take his canine companion and go into the woods. There he would make believe he was a soldier and set out to hunt his imaginary Japanese enemies. These fanciful journeys were always completed with the old Mauser rifle given to him by his father who had brought it back from the front lines of Europe when he fought in World War I.

Carlos also hunted at an early age with a .22-caliber J. C. Higgins single-shot rifle and would bring the animals he killed home to be cooked and fed to his struggling family. Inspired by his veteran father, Carlos Hathcock had dreamed of becoming a Marine all throughout his childhood. The stories of his father serving in Europe is what his imagination often built upon on when he went out on his adventures. And so, finally, on May 20, 1959, the day he turned 17 years old, he enlisted in the U.S. Marine Corps. Because he was only 17 years old, his mother sent written permission with him to the enlistment officers allowing him to join. They accepted him and he soon went off to training. Carlos Hathcock would go on to marry Josephine Bryan Winsted, known simply as "Jo", on the date of the Marine Corps birthday, on November 10, 1962, just three years later. Jo gave birth to a son, whom they named Carlos Norman Hathcock III, a son who would soon follow in his father's footsteps and was their only child.

From the beginning of his military career, his ability as a marksman was noted by everyone around him. His shooting skills were very quickly recognized by his instructors on the rifle range at Camp Pendleton where he would go to practice. He never stopped practicing. It was there at camp Pendleton that he was undergoing recruit training. After his recruit training was completed he was sent to Hawaii and, as a member of Company E, 2nd Battalion, 4th Marines, Carlos won the Pacific Division rifle championship. His skills in shooting long distances gained even more notoriety from his performance in that competition but his rise to shooting fame didn't stop there. After he had completed his assignment in Hawaii, Carlos Hathcock was sent to the Marine Air Station in Cherry Point, North Carolina. It wasn't long before his competitive nature and excellent marksmanship had him shooting competitively again.

On a notoriously tough shooting course, he nearly achieved a perfect score, something that had never been done before. During this competition, he set an all new Marine Corps record on the "A" Course ending with a score of 248 points out of a possible 250. His record hasn't been beaten even until today, though many have tried. Between these competitions, he of course continued his training and practiced shooting. Practice is something Carlos valued even more than natural talent. A few years later, he would win a competition that would make him even more infamous. The pinnacle of his competitive shooting career didn't occur until 1965. As a Lance Corporal, Carlos Hathcock entered and won a competition by out-shooting all of the over servicemen competing. Beating 3000 other servicemen, he won the coveted Wimbledon Cup at Camp Perry. Humorously, he didn't know he had won until minutes later after people began patting him on the back.

Shooting was not his only enhanced skill. His approach to, what is now called "stalking" in military vernacular but was what he called worming, was one of the greatest assets he took with him to war and is used in every branch of the military today. It is a fairly silent way of traversing fields of tall grass without being seen. His skill was his ability to crawl extremely close to the ground and make as small a trail behind him as possible. His "worming" would be used multiple times over his career but would most notably serve him in a 4 day 3 night mission at the end of his time in the war. He was extremely slim, standing 5 foot 10 inches tall and weighing only 120 pounds.

The year following his great win, in 1966, Carlos Hathcock was finally deployed to Vietnam, sent to serve as a military policeman. He was excited to finally serve as he had always imagined. Excelling at his position, he continued to strike awe in to those who were exposed to his marksmanship skills. He also adapted to the Marine, wartime life style with ease. Meanwhile Captain Edward James Land had been campaigning for the Marines to establish a position for snipers in every platoon. Finally getting his wish, Edward James Land began to recruit Marines to train as snipers, focusing his efforts on those who had set records in sharpshooting and were knowing for their precision. Of course, it wasn't long until he found Carlos Hathcock, and was especially impressed that he had won the Wimbledon Cup. Surely the man who had won the most prestigious prize for long-range shooting would make an excellent sniper. This unbeknownst to Carlos, this would begin his long and successful career.

He began training in Captain Edward James Land's newly established sniper program. Captain Land believed that the snipers he was training could have a large impact on their efforts in the war. And he was right. Once his training was completed, Carlos Hathcock began his new assignment as a Marine sniper, transferring to the 1st Marine Division Sniper Platoon. His platoon was operating out of Hill 55, which was positioned 35 miles South-West of Da Nang, Vietnam. Captain Jim Land's 17-man instructor team had trained at least 600 snipers in the 8 months between September 1966 and April 1967. By the end of that time, they were deadly. After completing their training they implemented their new skills and, during one 90-day period, the snipers had taken out more Viet Cong fighters than the entire local battalions had. It was then that Captain Land's group of snipers were dubbed "Murder Incorporated." Carlos Hathcock along with the other trained Marine snipers decided to renew an old Marine strategy which had been born and used in fight in the Pacific Islands in World War II. Their location was in the jungles of Vietnam and in these surroundings, he became an extremely easy target for the enemy North Vietnamese soldiers. So he decided to use this to his advantage. He would position himself and wait until he could spot his targets. Taking into consideration the air temperature, wind speed, and humidity he would prepare himself to shoot. He would see the flash of light that reflected off of their sniper rifle scopes and try to kill them before they shot at him. This cavalier and risky strategy is, in part, what led to him becoming known as the Vietnam War's deadliest sniper. Thanks to him and the adoption of this tactic, after only a short period of time the effects of the Marine snipers' strategy was sweeping through the area around Hill 55 and was felt by the North Vietnamese army.

It was here that Carlos Hathcock quickly began to rack a body count, though it was not possible to keep accurate track of each one. He did end up killing enough people to elicit a warrant on his head by the North Vietnamese. Through his impressive work as a sniper, he was promoted and became Sergeant Carlos Hathcock's reputation preceded him and was immediately recruited for multiple covert assignments. In the first of them, he was ordered to kill a French national who had been working for the North Vietnamese as an interrogator. He was responsible for torturing captured American airmen who were shot down.

Carlos Hathcock, with his exhaustive training and shooting skills was able to track the French interrogator and put just one round from his modified Winchester Model 70 sniper rifle into the Frenchman's career and his life. The second notable covert assignment that Sergeant Carlos Hathcock accepted was an assignment that seemed precarious at best. Instructed that his odds for survival were slim, Carlos Hathcock accepted and assignment with a North Vietnamese general as his target. Much like his make believe adventures as a child, he hunted the general and shot him a range of 800 yards, killing him. Much to everyone's surprise, Sergeant Carlos Hathcock returned to Hill 55 completely unscathed. And in a later covert assignment, Carlos Hathcock killed an enemy sniper after an intense back and forth between Carlos, with his spotter, and the North Vietnamese sniper. After an exchange of gunfire, the fatal round that killed the Vietnamese sniper was fired at 500 yards by Carlos Hathcock.

Sergeant Carlos Hathcock was always eager for work, requesting to be sent on a new mission as soon as his last one was over. He was once even confined to his room and forced to rest. His work was exhausting but thrilling. Captain Land, who had originally recruited and trained Hathcock described more of the uncomfortable parts of being a sniper. For instance, a sniper would need to remain seated or laying down for long periods, having to stay completely still and silent. And, if the enemy was around, any movement they made could attract attention and mean certain death. "A lot of times you would be sitting so long in one place you either urinated or defecated in your trousers," Land said once in an interview. Yet, Carlos Hathcock was passionate about being a skilled sniper. He loved his work not only because he was specifically adept at it, but because he felt very strongly that if he wasn't out their working, the enemy would have more chances to kill his fellow Marines. He didn't like the thought of killing another living breathing human being but he knew that he had to be the one to shoot first. "There was no second place in Vietnam...." He said. And he was right. There was only first place and dead.

Over his career, Carlos Hathcock had totaled 93 confirmed kills of North Vietnamese Army and Viet Cong personnel. In the Vietnam War there were regulations for Marines so sniper kills were required to be confirmed by an acting third party. The man confirming the kills needed to be an officer, and had to be someone besides the sniper's spotter. Of course, due to the nature of the sniper's work, they often did not have an acting third party present while they were shooting the enemies which made confirmation difficult. This was especially true if the target was behind enemy lines and the sniper needed to sneak past the lines to kill, as was usually the case. When asked for his number, Carlos Hathcock estimated that he had actually killed between 300 and 400 enemy fighters during deployment in Vietnam but wasn't able to confirm them for obvious reasons. He had learned over his career that the best times for sniping the enemy was at sunrise or sunset. At sunset, the enemy fighters would be tired from their patrol and would let their guard down. The same could be said about them in the mornings. They would not be awake enough yet to pay attention to details and would miss things. He would watch them coming and going, smoking cigarettes, and joking with each other. They never saw his bullets coming, feeling naïvely safe in their camps.

Sergeant Hathcock's kills had made enough of an impact that the North Vietnamese Army eventually put out a bounty of $30,000 on Hathcock's head. He was well known throughout the enemy ranks for killing so many of their men. He was viewed as so detrimental that even though rewards for U.S. snipers by the North Vietnamese soldiers typically ranged from $8 to $2,000. However, Carlos Hathcock's career had preceded him and therefore he now held the record for highest bounty placed on a United States soldier's head. They knew that the deadliest sniper they were fighting needed the largest bounty. They had hoped that the large reward for his head would inspire someone to kill him quickly. The bounty, of course, failed to intimidate Carlos Hathcock and he killed every single Vietnamese marksman who came after him to collect the enormous bounty. It was at around this time that Carlos received a nickname that would be attributed to him for the rest of his life. Wearing a white feather on him at all times, the Viet Cong and North Vietnamese Army called Sergeant Hathcock "Du kích Lông Trắng" which, translated into English, means "White Feather Sniper".

He was known to have kept it in a band on his bush hat even on his missions. It was almost like a dare to those looking for him, as if to say "here I am". In fact, it was known that Sergeant Carlos Hathcock only removed the white feather one time in his entire deployment. It was when he had to crawl approximately 1,500 yards on his side through a field. He decided not to crawl flat on his stomach because he knew that it would make a wider "slug trail" or indentation of where he had crawled. He was sent on a mission to kill a high-ranking officer in the North Vietnamese Army. He was not informed of the details of the mission until after he accepted it. After four days and three nights of sneaking and crawling inch by inch and not sleeping or eating, his mission was successful. His "worming" tactic was solidified as an efficient tool in covert missions.

During the mission, Carlos Hathcock reported later, that he was almost stepped on by the enemy multiple times when he was laying on the ground. Dressed in camouflage with grass and vegetation around him in a meadow just shortly after the sun had set he waited and inched his way along. At another point on his mission, he was almost bitten by a bamboo viper snake, but fortunately he had the presence of mind to remain still so he wouldn't end up giving up his position. After a long stare down between Hathcock and the snake, the snake flicked its tongue and slithered off into the tall grass. Carefully, Hathcock had let out a silent sigh of relief. On one of the days he was in the meadow, he had military trucks, known as Twin 51s, roll past him on each side. His position was precarious at best and many thought he wouldn't make it back. Finally, as the target, the high ranking officer left his encampment, Carlos Hathcock fired his rifle and a single shot flew through the air and struck the officer in the chest, killing him within minutes. As soon as the man fell, everyone began running past him to get to the trees for cover. Once he had completed his mission, he crawled back to the tree line before he stood up and ran, careful to watch for traps as he ran to his extraction point.

His extreme patience and dedication are what set him apart from the rest of the snipers and ultimately made him the infamous sniper he is known as today. Waiting in stealth for the right moment, Sergeant Carlos Hathcock also once shot a Chinese army officer out of a small boat at a distance of around 300 yards in another incident. He then watched the officer drown in the river. Captain Land noted it as odd and said it was telling about Hathcock's personality because Carlos Hathcock didn't mention it when he had his debriefing session. It was a job for him. It was just what he did.

After his success in killing their high ranking official, the North Vietnamese Army grew impatient and irate. Sergeant Carlos Hathcock or "White Feather" had been a thorn in their side for too long and was becoming too large of a liability. So they decided to send a platoon of Vietnamese snipers to hunt down "White Feather" Carlos Hathcock and kill him to end his reign of terror in their area. Alerted to the plan, the Marines banded together and many of the Marines in his area donned white feathers in their bush hats to trick the Vietnamese snipers into thinking they were the target. Though risking their own lives, these Marines knew how big of an impact Carlos Hathcock's death would have on the fight in the area. The deception worked. Throughout his entire career, Carlos Hathcock was never shot. This was an incredible feat for someone who had done as many missions as he had and had been deployed for as long as he had. But of course he often came close to the spiraling bullets around him.

As mentioned earlier, one of Sergeant Hathcock's most famous accomplishments was shooting and killing an enemy sniper through his own rifle scope, hitting him in the eye and killing him instantly. Carlos Hathcock and a fellow marine named John Roland Burke, acting as his spotter, had been stalking the enemy sniper through the jungle in the area of Hill 55, which was the base from which Hathcock was operating in the southwest of Da Nang. The sniper they were stalking, who was known only as the "Cobra", had already killed several Marines as he made his way through the area and was thought to have been sent on a mission to kill Carlos Hathcock. When the Marines had received intelligence that the Cobra was after him, the men Carlos Hathcock reported to suggested that they either move him to a different base or to not send him out on missions for the time being. But of course, Carlos Hathcock knew that he would be the best person to stop the Cobra and set out to kill him first. The Cobra had killed one of the gunnery men outside Hathcock's door which angered him. As they followed him and tracked his movements, Sergeant Hathcock got the opportunity he was waiting for and it was purely by chance. Hathcock had tripped over a log and made a sound. Cobra had heard it and fired a shot, striking Hathcock's spotter's water canteen. It was then that the Cobra started to run and try to hide somewhere else but unfortunately for him, he was facing the sun. Crouching in the jungle, Carlos Hathcock saw a flash of light which was the sunlight reflecting off of the Cobra's scope off in the bushes. Sergeant Hathcock aimed his sniper rifle and fired at it. He shot and his bullet went through the scope, killing the sniper.

Once his bullet struck, Carlos Hathcock went over to survey the area he had suspected Cobra to be in. Once he found the body and saw where his bullet had struck, Hathcock concluded that what must have happened was that his bullet went straight down the enemy's own scope, hitting him in his eye, because both snipers, he and the Cobra, were aiming at each other at the same time and luckily excellent marksmen Sergeant Hathcock fired first. The other sniper only had a few seconds to act but failed to do so. Technically, taking into consideration the flight time of rounds at such long ranges, both snipers could have actually simultaneously killed one another. However, the other sniper failed to strike Hathcock. As a prize for his kill, Carlos Hathcock decided to take the dead sniper's rifle, hoping to bring it back home as his "trophy". Unfortunately, after he returned to base, put it in the armory and tagged it, it was stolen.

In 1966, Sergeant Carlos Hathcock was sent on another covert mission, this time the target was a female Viet Cong sniper. She was also a platoon commander and interrogator. Known as "Apache", she was ruthless and so well-known because of her methods for torturing captured U.S. Marines and the South Vietnamese Army troops. After she tortured them she would leave them and let them bleed to death. "Apache" was a very high profile target and was monitored by Military Intelligence. "Apache" was not only known for savagely torturing captives but was especially known for torturing prisoners within earshot of U.S. military bases. Reportedly Sergeant Hathcock later told other officers that one of Apache's trademark torturing tactic was to cut off her victim's eyelids which she then kept them as souvenirs. She was also known to have often castrated her captives and skinned another captive alive. Flanked by her own sniper platoon, she was able to cause massive amounts of damage. After skinning the kid Marine alive, she let him go and he ran into the sight of Hathcock who was on their bunker at the time and he died there. Hathcock then looked for his opening. After a lower ranking enemy soldier saw them Hathcock and his fellow Marines, he ran back to report to Apache. Soon after, she and 4 men approached, running towards Sergeant Hathcock. Through one of the men she was with tried to stop her, she continued one until a bullet stopped her in her tracks. She was killed by Sergeant Carlos Hathcock with the help of Captain Edward James Land. He fired one bullet which killed her and shot a second one for good measure. After seeing the damage she had caused, this kill was personal and it was the one he spoke most passionately about. This kill was also considered a major morale victory for the US troops because the woman named "Apache" was so successful at terrorizing and torturing the troops in the area of the Hill 55 base.

Sergeant Carlos Hathcock was not only famous for his skills and technique but has also had an influence on the type of artillery used by Marines in war zones. The 50 caliber machine gun, along with the same type of scope Carlos used mounted on it became an impressive tool for killing enemy soldiers. The first time he used the two together, he had been instructed to test it by Captain Land. After constructing a pseudo mountain for him to perch on, Hathcock took over the gun and began scouting through his scope to watch the movements and activities of the enemies. He did this for three days and, on the third day, he took 3 shots to get used to it and test what it could do. He noted that the shortest shot was 1000 yards, the furthest was 2500 yards. The he had it zeroed in. Just after that, Carlos Hathcock got lucky. An enemy soldier, nicknamed hamburger, a man who had been an aide to the "Apache" before she died, walked right into his path and stopped to get a drink.

Carlos aimed and shot at the exact moment Hamburger stood up and hit him.

At another point in his time in Vietnam, Carlos Hathcock took part in what is referred to as the five day engagement. An entire troop of brand new, North Vietnamese Army soldiers approached Hathcock and his fellow Marines. Untrained and unaware, the troop approached them through the center of a valley. This was a position that was easily seen by Carlos Hathcock and the other Marines. Sergeant Hathcock immediately shot the leading officer and his spotter took out the officer in the back leaving only one remaining leader. The last officer held strong for only a few more moments as the Marines killed two more men and then turned and ran. The remaining men were more fearless and remained there. Carlos Hathcock had already doled out his three shots, after which it is customary for a sniper to leave. It was then that he made a decision. The enemy remained so Hathcock and his men stayed as well. Some of the North Vietnamese soldiers tried to break from behind but Hathcock was too quick and they killed them. Then they moved position, unbeknownst to the enemy. It wasn't long before the North Vietnamese soldiers attacked the position Carlos Hathcock and the other Marines had held originally. This gave the Marines an easy target to kill more of them.

After his long deployment in the humid jungles of Vietnam, Sergeant Carlos Hathcock was finally able to return to the United States in 1967. But his training and skills had been hardwired into his nature and he missed being a part of the Marine Corps. So he returned to Vietnam in 1969, and he took command of a platoon of snipers. Finally feeling back at home, he continued to train the platoon until an unexpected and horrible accident. It was on September 16, 1969. Sergeant Carlos Hathcock was riding the AMTRAC along Route 1, North of LZ Baldy base, and the AMTRAC, an LVT-5, suddenly hit an anti-tank mine and his career as a sniper came to an end. After the blast, Carlos Hathcock managed to pull seven Marines from the flame-engulfed vehicle, endangering himself in the process. He, of course, suffered severe burns to the extent that some were even third-degree burns, which covered parts of his face, trunk, arms and legs. This totaled about 90 percent of his body. But once he had rescued the others, he was able to jump to safety and wait until help arrived.

All eight of the injured Marines were evacuated to a hospital ship called USS Repose for recovery. They were then sent to a Naval Hospital in Tokyo, Japan then ultimately to a burn center at Brooke Army Medical Center in San Antonio, Texas. He was hospitalized and had more than 13 skin grafts. And while he was recovering, he was awarded the Purple Heart metal though he tried to refuse it at the time. That was not the only metal that would be awarded to him. Over his career he was also awarded these metals: Navy Commendation Medal[1], Achievement Medal[2], Good Conduct Medal[3], National Defense Service Medal[4], Vietnam Service Medal[5], Gallantry Cross[6], and the Vietnam Campaign Medal[7]. Almost 30 years later, he received a Silver Star for this bravery in the accident and saving his fellow Marines.

After the war and his recovery, Carlos Hathcock put his energy into helping establish the Marine Corps Scout Sniper School, at the Marine base in Quantico, Virginia. Unfortunately his heroic actions in the AMTRAC accident, he retained severe injuries and he was in nearly constant pain. But he refused to give in to his pain, so he continued to dedicate himself to teaching snipers ad the Scout Sniper School in Quantico. But in 1975, Sergeant Carlos Hathcock's health began to get worse. The doctors at the U.S. Naval Hospital at

---

1.   https://en.wikipedia.org/wiki/Navy_and_Marine_Corps_Commendation_Medal

2.   https://en.wikipedia.org/wiki/Achievement_Medal

3.   https://en.wikipedia.org/wiki/Good_Conduct_Medal_(United_States)

4.   https://en.wikipedia.org/wiki/National_Defense_Service_Medal

5.   https://en.wikipedia.org/wiki/Vietnam_Service_Medal

6.   https://en.wikipedia.org/wiki/Gallantry_Cross_(Vietnam)

7.   https://en.wikipedia.org/wiki/Vietnam_Campaign_Medal

Portsmouth, VA ran tests were ultimately able to give a diagnosis. Carlos Hathcock was diagnosed with multiple sclerosis, an illness from which he would never recover. It was an incurable degenerative nerve disorder. Yet his passion for duty remained and he stayed in the Marine Corps. His health continued to decline but he continued on as long as he could. When he was just 55 days shy of his 20 year anniversary of service, a milestone that would have made him eligible for retirement wages, he was issued a permanent disability separation from the Marine Corps. Him being medically discharged from service, allowed him to receive 100 percent disability pay from the Marines which was fortunate because he would have received only 50 percent of his final pay grade if had he retired under regular circumstances after his 20 year milestone.

At his retirement ceremony, he was given a plaque made by his commanding officer. It read: "There have been many Marines. And there have been many Marine marksmen. But there is only one Marine Sniper—Gunnery Sgt. Carlos N. Hathcock II. One Shot—One Kill." Which serve to signify how extraordinary his service had been.

Once discharged, Carlos Hathcock felt as though his purpose was taken. He became depressed because he felt and believed that the Marines had kicked him out without truly honoring his contributions. His state of depression was difficult to take and his wife Jo Winstead-Hathcock almost ended up leaving him, but after true consideration she decided to stay and help him to work through it. It was fortunate that she did. Discharged Sergeant Carlos Hathcock continued to suffer but he eventually found enjoyment in a hobby. It was the hobby of shark fishing, which ultimately helped him overcome his bout of depression. Carlos Hathcock also found fulfillment when he was able to provide sniper instruction to police departments and certain select military units, notably the SEAL Team Six. He of course is still remembered to this day by the men he trained. "He emphasized that snipers could not be John Wayne, that we should be more reserved,"

William Bartholomew said. He was a former sniper with the Baltimore Police Department. It was for an article that would be published in The Baltimore Sun. William Bartholomew described Sergeant Hathcock's training methods as such: "If you didn't apply what he taught you, if you made an absentminded error, he could stare right through you. He could chew you out without ever raising his voice." Unfortunately, it wasn't too long before he was confined to a wheelchair and unable to demonstrate his tactics to the trainees.

Carlos Hathcock was known as a hero. He was interviewed a lot about his escapades as the years went by. In one interview he said that he was able to survive and thrive in his work because he had an innate ability to "get in the bubble" as he called it which meant that he was able to put himself into a state of "utter, complete, absolute concentration". He practiced this exercise first with his equipment and riffles and then began to implement this into his environment and surroundings. In this state, every breeze and every leaf meant something to him. Though his fellow Marines were well trained in sinking into the environment, Carlos Hathcock brought this to a whole new level.

When the war was over and Sergeant Hathcock had returned home, a friend of his showed Carlos Hathcock a passage of a book written by Ernest Hemingway which read: "Certainly there is no hunting like the hunting of man, and those who have hunted armed men long enough and like it, never really care for anything else thereafter." He apparently copied Ernest Hemingway's words down on a piece of paper. He then said "He got that right, It was the hunt, not the killing." He felt as though this passage embodied his approach to his career and how he had felt about being a sniper. Later, Carlos Hathcock said in a biography that was written about his career: "I like shooting, and I love hunting. But I never did enjoy killing anybody. It's my job. If I don't get those bastards, then they're gonna kill a lot of these kids dressed up like Marines. That's the way I look at it." This quote revealed the softer side of the well-known, highly skilled assassin.

When questioned about if he liked killing, he responded by saying that you would have to be crazy to want to run around a jungle killing people. He did it to protect his fellow Marines, not for sport.

Carlos Hathcock and Jo Winstead-Hathcock's son, named Carlos Hathcock III, decided to follow in his father's footsteps and when he was old enough he enlisted in the U.S. Marine Corps. After a successful career, he retired from the Marine Corps with the status of a Gunnery Sergeant matching his father. After his career as a shooter, he became a member of the Board of Governors in the Marine Corps Distinguished Shooters Association. Sadly, Sergeant Carlos Norman Hathcock II died on February 22, 1999, at the age of 57 in Virginia Beach, Virginia. His long fight with Multiple sclerosis was over. He died from complications resulting from his multiple sclerosis leaving behind his wife Jo and his son Carlos Hathcock III who mourned him deeply. After his death, a representative of a local Native American tribe was invited to Hathcock's funeral. He presented some eagle feathers to Jo Hathcock and her son, Carlos Hathcock III; and also presented feathers to Hathcock's long time shooting buddy, Captain Jim Land. The Native Americans of that tribe had respected Hathcock as a lone warrior, who was part Native American himself. He is buried at Woodlawn Memorial Gardens in Norfolk, Virginia.

To honor him after his death, a variant of the M25 Rifle was named after him, called the White Feather. This rifle was used in the Gulf wars and is still used frequently by the military today. And because he was such a well-known and respected sniper, there have been many biographies written about him including *Marine Sniper: 93 Confirmed Kills and White feather: Carlos Hathcock USMC scout sniper: an authorized biographical memoir.* His legacy lives on even in films such as "The Sniper" and "Saving Private Ryan" where his tactics and strategies were imitated. Characters in shows like Criminal Minds: Suspect Behavior, JAG and NCIS are modeled after Carlos Hathcock and his exploits are still referred in many crime and military dramas. The main character of Stephen Hunter's Bob Lee Swagger thriller book series, are loosely based on Sergeant Carlos Hathcock II. Even the main character's name is Gunny Sergeant Carl Hitchcock". Sergeant Carlos Hathcock also remains a legend in the Marines both in training measures and is immortalized in landmarks. For instance, the Carlos Hathcock Award is presented every year to the Marine who is deemed to have done the most to promote marksmanship. Hathcock also has a sniper range named for Him at Camp LeJeune, N.C. and on March 9, 2007, the rifle and pistol complex at Marine Corps Air Station Miramar[8] was officially renamed the Carlos Hathcock Range Complex in his honor.

---

8.   https://en.wikipedia.org/wiki/Marine_Corps_Air_Station_Miramar

DON STEINBRUNNER : COUNTRY OVER FOOTBALL

85

DONALD GIVENS

Country Over Football – the Story of Major Donald T. Steinbrunner

Major Donald T. Steinbrunner was a successful professional football player in the 1950's. Drafted by the Cleveland Browns, he was an offensive tackle who got lots of playing time during his rookie (and only) season with the NFL. During that time, he'd have the opportunity to play in the NFL Championship game between the Cleveland Browns and the Detroit Lions. Before the next season however, Steinbrunner would be off the gridiron and serving his country as an officer in the United States Air Force. He would later be sent to Vietnam resulting in his death at the young age of 35.

The Early Years

Born in 1932, Don was one of two children born to John and Florence Steinbrunner. He grew up on a medium-size farm in Acme (Whatcom County), Washington. Growing up in a rural community, he was an outdoorsman and enjoyed playing all sorts of sports. He later attended Mount Baker High School in Deming, Washington where he lettered and was an all-state athlete in both basketball and football. In 1948, head coaches came together to choose the state's all-star football team. Steinbrunner was one of the players chosen for the team along with other leading football players from the state of Washington. Steinbrunner graduated from high school in 1949.

College Career

Although he had many colleges pursuing him, Steinbrunner chose to attend Washington State College (now Washington State University) in Pullman, about a six hour's drive from his hometown. At the collegiate level, he continued to play double sports, and being a born leader, became captain for both teams. During his freshman year, he excelled on the court averaging over 3 points per game. He also played two positions, linebacker and offensive lineman while on the Cougar's football team. It was on the football squad that he made the most impact. Along with being a three-year letter winner, he received all-conference recognition and made the all-Coast defensive team in his sophomore year. He had many successes and achievements in his collegiate career as a tackler and offensive lineman. As a result, he garnered the attention of many teams in the National Football League.

Along with playing sports, he took an interest in military education and joined the universities Air Force ROTC (Reserved Officer Training Corp) program. He would complete his studies and receive his degree from Washington State College in 1953. Along with his degree, he'd also become a commissioned military officer upon graduation.

Drafted By the Cleveland Browns

The same year of his college graduation, Don Steinbrunner would get the call of a lifetime when drafted to play in the National Football League. Having had a successful career in college football, he would continue to play as an offensive tackle with the Cleveland Browns who had selected him in the sixth round of the draft. His performance at training camp however would prove to be a little disappointing to the coaching staff. Consequently, they'd cut him from the team seemingly ending his hopes of playing in the NFL. Nonetheless, after their starting tackle had an injury just a few games into the season's start, they would recall Steinbrunner and sign him to sign a contract for the remainder of the season.

In his first year of play, the Cleveland Browns had an exceptional season going so far as to win the Eastern Conference. Traveling to the NFL Championships, they'd face the Detroit Lions who would defeat them in the end by only one point. Wearing the number 74, despite his lack of experience, Steinbrunner got some playing time. But after just one season in the NFL, his career path would change when called to active duty.

Active Military Service

To fulfill the two-year commitment he made to military service while in college, Steinbrunner went active duty in 1954, early in the Vietnam conflict. The plan was for him to finish the two years and return to football and the Cleveland Browns. Coach Paul Brown, who was very fond of Steinbrunner, had kept him on their roster. Nonetheless, he'd recommit to the Air Force instead as he was happy with military life. Steinbrunner was also concerned about his ability to perform in professional football due to a recurring knee injury.

Steinbrunner spent much of his military career at the U.S. Air Force Academy in Colorado Springs. However, at the beginning of his career, he chose to train to become a policemen at Westover Air Force Base in Massachusetts. After a while, having a passion for flying, he decided to expand his skills in the area of navigation. As a navigator, he was skilled in planning air strikes or conventional bombing attacks.

After having served in the Air Force stateside for over a decade, the conflict in Vietnam heightened and Steinbrunner voluntarily accepted a deployment. He traveled with the 315th Air Commando Group (also known as the Ranch Hands) and would spend the next several months flying missions over South Vietnam. Being 34 years of age at the time and having been in the military for over a decade, Steinbrunner did not have to go to Vietnam but chose to go anyway.

Being a family man, he struggled with the decision to leave his wife and children. Nonetheless, he wanted to go because he strongly believed in the mission of the war. He also believed it his duty as a seasoned military leader to take his experience to Vietnam to help train the younger officers. Within just a few short months of serving in Vietnam, he was shot in the knee during a flying mission. Consequently, his superiors suggested he go home or recommended he take a lighter, less dangerous assignment. Being committed and wanting to complete what he started, Steinbrunner declined both offers and continued his work in Vietnam as an Air Force navigator.

At the time of his death, Steinbrunner held the rank of Major in the United States Air Force.

Coaching Football at the Air Force Academy

Because of his football knowledge and skills, Steinbrunner would also serve as assistant football coach for four seasons with the Air Force Academy in Colorado. Successful in his role due to his experience and outgoing personality, he was a great recruiter and mentor for the players. The Air Force Academy Falcons became like a second family to both Steinbrunner and his young kids. Often the Cadets would come to the family home for meals or to review gameday film. The Steinbrunner kids would also look forward to Saturday games at the Academy when they could enjoy watching the games with other fans. In a fall 1963 issue of the <u>Colorado Springs Gazette</u>, Steinbrunner's son David became a feature story while attending a football match against the University of Washington. This short article included a photo of David running on the field in a football uniform – cleats and all.

During his tenure as assistant football coach, the Air Force Academy had many memorable achievements including a trip to the Gator Bowl in 1963.

Family of Don Steinbrunner

Steinbrunner married his wife Meredyth after a chance meeting on the campus of Case Western Reserve University in the Cleveland area. Meredyth was a medical student there and Steinbrunner was taking courses at the college while on break from the Cleveland Browns. Tall and handsome with a nice smile, he was extremely charming and it didn't take long for him to win her heart.

Shortly after marrying, they had three children - two girls and one boy. At the time of his death, his son David was 11, the daughter Diane 7 and Wendy even younger. When speaking about their dad, they remember him as being warm, caring and overall a great father and husband. He was the type of dad who would play outdoors in the snow with the children and put them inside his coat when they were cold.

Don's wife Meredyth and kids remained in Colorado Springs after his death. They were quiet for quite a while about their dad and husband as many were still protesting or criticizing the war. Now many years later, his son David who remembers him most is now a landscaper in that same town. He says he often runs across people who recognize the name and acknowledge his dad's heroism which fills him with lots of pride.

Along with his wife and children, Steinbrunner was survived by both his mom and sister Lee. His father preceded him in death.

Killed Flying Over Kontum

On July 20, 1967, Steinbrunner was aboard the UC-123B aircraft leading an herbicidal warfare mission. The mission entailed spraying Agent Orange over Kontum in South Vietnam. Shot down while in flight, the aircraft would crash and eventually catch afire killing Steinbrunner along with the pilot, co-pilot and other crew members instantly.

Had he lived, Steinbrunner would have returned to the states and his family before the Christmas season. Instead, his family would receive his remains as they were shipped back to Washington for burial.

Burial

Buried at the United States Air Force Academy Cemetery, Major Donald Steinbrunner's grave is marked with a simple headstone. All gray, this tombstone includes a small cross signifying his faith along with his name, date of birth and date of death. His rank of Major in the United States Air Force is also included.

At Saxon Cemetery in his birth/hometown of Acme, Washington, there is also a memorial there for Steinbrunner. This is where both his mom and dad are also buried.

Heroism Unknown

For well over a decade, most believed Bob Kalsu was the only professional football player to have died in Vietnam. Perhaps this was because Steinbrunner had been away from professional football for many years prior to his death. Also, Kalsu had been Rookie of the Year with the NFL which gave him a lot more notoriety in professional sports. Truth is however, Steinbrunner died a few years before Kalsu making him the first NFL player to die in the Vietnam War.

Kalsu himself was not well-known until <u>Sports Illustrated</u> published a story about him in 2001. The article talked about Kalsu's heroism and mentioned a display about him on exhibition at the Pro Football Hall of Fame located in Canton, Ohio. Unfortunately, the article wrongfully said Kalsu was the only NFL player to have died in Vietnam. Although the NFL records accurately said Steinbrunner had been killed in Vietnam, it seemed most had overlooked his name and only knew of Kalsu. Obviously when doing his research, the <u>Sports Illustrated</u> reporter also missed it. Nonetheless, that would change when the Steinbrunner's caught wind of the story. Once brought to their attention, they contacted the museum administrators to request a correction and to speak of their loved one, Major Donald T. Steinbrunner who died in Vietnam in 1967. The entire Steinbrunner family was happy to hear of the story about Kalsu; nonetheless, they simply wanted the same recognition for their loved one.

After meeting with the family, museum administrators were excited to pay tribute to both men. A special opening for the exhibit and a ceremony honoring both Kalsu and Steinbrunner took place at the Pro Football Hall of Fame on Veteran's Day, 2001. Attended by over 200 people, Steinbrunner's wife Meredyth, daughters Wendy and Diane and son David were all there. Part of a permanent display entitled "Football and America", the exhibit strives to educate the public about Kalsu and Steinbrunner, their life and choice to serve over football. It also features items on loan from the family including his Purple Heart and Browns' football helmet. Of course it was a big sacrifice for Steinbrunner's family to depart with these treasured heirlooms, but they are encouraged to know that many from all over the world will share in their husband/dad's life through these personal treasures.

What Would He Have Done Had He Lived

Entertaining the idea of Steinbrunner returning to the NFL, while in Vietnam, Coach Brown of the Cleveland Browns would keep him on the roster. Steinbrunner however had different dreams. He enjoyed military life and would sign up for another tour after his two-year commitment was complete. In total, he'd end up serving 13 years in the United States Air Force before his passing.

After his tour in Vietnam, Steinbrunner planned to continue his military career once returning home to Colorado Springs. He also hoped to return to his role of coaching at the Air Force Academy. An inspirational leader and teacher, he had aspirations of coaching football possibly at the collegiate or professional level after retiring from the military. Nonetheless, because of his death, it was not to be.

Vietnam Veterans Memorial Wall, Purple Heart and Distinguished Flying Cross Award

The name of Major Donald T. Steinbrunner is included with the names of many other heroes on the Veterans Memorial Wall in Washington, D.C. Having his name engraved on this national monument, Steinbrunner will always have a permanent place in history.

After his death, Steinbrunner would receive both the Purple Heart and Distinguished Flying Cross Award in honor of his bravery and selfless sacrifice. The Distinguished Flying Cross Award is a medal presented to aerial officers or enlisted military airmen who have shown acts of heroism. A bronze medal with a cross design and service ribbon, its opposite side is engraved with Steinbrunner's name and rank in the United States Air Force. The Purple Heart is a military decoration awarded by declaration of the President to soldiers wounded or killed in battle. Heart shaped with a gold border, it also features a purple ribbon. The family received and the son David presented with both awards in a private military ceremony directed by a United States Air Force General.

Part of the citation for the Purple Heart presented posthumously to Steinbrunner reads as follows:

"Disregarding the hazards of flying the difficult target terrain and the opposition presented by hostile ground forces, he led the formation through one attack and returned to make a second attack. The outstanding heroism and selfless devotion to duty displayed by Major Steinbrunner reflect great credit upon himself and the United States Air Force."

Other military rewards Steinbrunner has received for his bravery include the National Defense Service Award, Vietnam Campaign Medal and the Vietnam Service Medal.

Honored by the Cleveland Browns

In November, 2004, Steinbrunner's beloved Cleveland Browns paid tribute to him during a pre-football game celebration. The Browns invited all servicemen and women to attend a game against the Pittsburgh Steelers and asked them to come in uniform. Also in attendance was his widow Meredyth along with all three of their children.

Throughout the years, the Cleveland Browns have attempted to honor not just Steinbrunner, but other players, coaches and administrators who have served in the Armed Forces. One such event held to honor these vets included a Memorial Day contest in which fans were challenged to match players with the military branch in which they served. The winner received an autograph player's photograph and other Browns' team goodies. Steinbrunner of course was one of the players included in the contest questions.

Along with the National Football League, each year during the Veteran's Day weekend, the Browns will take time from the game to salute fallen heroes from all of the wars. Steinbrunner always has a special place in that ceremony because he once played for the Cleveland Browns.

Pro Football Hall of Fame Traveling Exhibit

In 2014, the Pro Football Hall of Fame created another exhibit to honor Steinbrunner and other professional football players who'd served in the Armed Forces. This one would travel to museums and football stadiums across the country. Both educational and inspirational, it tells the story of how the NFL has impacted life during World War II, Vietnam and the Gulf Wars. Many personal mementos from heroes like Steinbrunner are part of the exhibit. NFL films and various photographs are also included in this over 2000 square foot exhibit. Entitled "Pro Football and the American Spirit: The NFL and the U.S. Armed Force", other NFL players, coaches and administrators honored in the exhibit include Pat Tillman, Bob Kalsu, Art Donovan and General Earnest Cheatham.

Making stops at numerous museums, it has previously been on display at the Gerald R. Ford Museum in Grand Rapids, Michigan, the Kansas Sports Hall of Fame in Wichita, Kansas and the Haggin Museum in Stockton, California. Many football stadiums including the Hall at Patriot Place (home of the New England Patriots) have also hosted the exhibit to share with fans and stadium guests.

40th Anniversary

Held in the summer of 2007, 40 years after the death of Steinbrunner, there was a memorial celebration at the United States Air Force Academy in his honor. Coordinated by his son David and personnel from the academy, along with honoring his dad's memory, the celebration brought together Steinbrunner's teammates from high school, college and the Cleveland Browns to share fond memories. Also attended by many Vietnam veterans, it provided a chance for many to meet and reconnect.

Other Honorariums

Since the Pro Football Hall of Fame acknowledged Don Steinbrunner, other sports and military organizations have also honored him in various ways. A few of these include Memorial Day and Veteran's Day tributes hosted by the National Football League along with tributes at the United States Air Force Academy and the Pentagon at an annual Vietnam War Commemoration ceremony.

Washington State University also has its own Veteran's Memorial wall located in the center of the campus. This wall pays tribute to staff, faculty and alumni of the university who have served and/or gave their lives for freedom. Engraved on a plaque in the Vietnam section of the memorial, you'll find the name of Major Donald T. Steinbrunner, an alum from the class of 1953.

Steinbrunner's story has also been included in numerous books such as <u>When Football Went to War</u> by Todd Anton and Bill Nowlin. Newspapers such as <u>USA Today</u> and the <u>New York Daily News</u> have also featured stories on Donald Steinbrunner and how he chose country over football.

Gordon & Shughart : American Heroes

Patrick Lawson

Gary Gordon was a Master Sergeant in the U.S. Army while his brother-in-arms, Randy Shughart, was a Sergeant First class.

Both men were non-commissioned officers in the United States Army's elite special operations unit, the 1st Special Forces Operational Detachment Delta which is more commonly known as "Delta Force."

After witnessing one of the Black Hawk helicopters shot down by Somali rebels, both soldiers volunteered to insert themselves on the ground to rescue any remaining survivors. Facing a growing angry mob armed with gunfire, Gordon and Shughart valiantly battled to save their fellow soldiers.

Both men were awarded the Medal of Honor posthumously for their actions during the Battle of Mogadishu in October of 1993. Their acts of courage were later made into a movie called "Black Hawk Down."

EARLY LIFE

Gary Gordon was born August 30th, 1960 in Lincoln, Maine.

Gary would graduate from Mattanawcook Academy in 1978. He would enlist in the U.S. Army that same year at age 18, arriving at basic training on December 4th, 1978.

Gary's personality has been described as shy and withdrawn. "There's all this speculation about Gary," Mike Murchison said, a childhood friend. "About who he was and how he came to be that way. How can anybody really know? He was so damned quiet. He never really told us anything at all."

But the questions remain. Given Gary's later acts of valor and courage, where did his sense of duty and sacrifice come from? Why risk his life for soldiers that he never met?

"It is this town of Lincoln," Senator Olympia Snowe said. "It is the quintessential small town that has forged the fabric of a great American. He represented America's small towns' ideals and values, and the town where he grew up."

Gordon trained as a combat engineer and became a Special Forces Engineer with the 2nd Battalion of the 10th Special Forces Group. He would marry his wife Carmen and the couple would have two children.

In December of 1986, eight years after enlisting in the Army, Gary was picked to join the 1st Special Forces Operational Detachment or Delta Force.

During his tenure in Delta Force, Gordon advanced to Team Sergeant.

"Both Gordon and Shughart have commonalities in their childhoods," military historian Bill Donovan said. "They both grew up in cities named Lincoln, Gary in Maine and Randy in Nebraska. They both grew up in small towns where the sense of American values stood firm. Gordon grew up in a town where there were less than four thousand people at the time. He grew up in a place where there was a sense of community, a duty to serve your fellow man. Values like those would shape the soldier that he would become."

Randall Shughart was born on August 13th, 1958 in Lincoln, Nebraska. He was born into a military family as his father, Herbert, was an Air Force officer. After his father retired from service, he moved the family to Newville, Pennsylvania to live off a dairy farm. Randy tended the herd and farmed along with his brother and two sisters.

"Again, Newville was a very small town," Donovan said. "Less than two thousand people. Working on a farm and in such a small community, Shughart wasn't exposed to the counter-culture ideas of the 1970s. He was brought up with a sense of duty and hard work which allowed him to become not only a successful soldier but an elite one."

Shughart made a decision to join the Army early on while attending Big Spring High School in Newville. He entered the service upon graduating and completed AIT (advanced individual training), Airborne School and was then assigned to the 2nd Ranger Battalion, 75th Ranger Regiment at Fort Lewis, Washington.

"Shughart did the ranger thing. He went into SURT which was short for Small Unit Ranger Tactics and with that he was able to gain entry into Ranger school. He earned the Ranger tab but then leave active duty for a spell and enter the Reserves in 1980."

Three years later, however, Shughart would return to active duty and enter Special Forces training. He would be assigned to "Delta Force" and serve out of Fort Bragg, North Carolina.

Shughart would be promoted to Assistant Team Sergeant.

"Delta Force is an elite force that is neither confirmed or denied by the United States military," Donovan said. "Their missions are highly classified and obviously, they've done things that we in the general public will never know about. But the fact that both Shughart and Gordon were a part of this elite squad tells you just about everything you need to know about their character, both mental and physical. The physical requirements to even be considered to be part of the Delta Force unit is more rigorous than an Iron Man competition. Then there is a battery of psychological exams that the men must go through, they are interrogated to the point of a mental breakdown. Two hundred fifty may be selected but only five percent will actually survive the training process. Gordon and Shughart were the elite of the elite, make no mistake about it."

SOMALIA

"War-torn Somalia" would become a media catch phrase by the late 1980s. Different armed rebel groups began to resist the Siad Barre regime in power and in 1991 these groups managed to overthrow the government.

"There was never supposed to be a war in Somalia," Donovan said. "Bush the first sent our troops over as peacekeepers. They were supposed to bring aid and food to the starving people of Somalia. This would help, to some extent, but the warlords would steal the food. Then Clinton took power and the mission turned from merely extending humanitarian aid to restoring a government."

With no governing authority in place, numerous clans began fighting for control. This forced the United Nations to send troops in as peacekeepers.

But when Gordon and Shughart were assigned to Mogadishu, it was not part of a peacekeeping mission of any kind.

"Mohamed Farrah Aidid had emerged had the most ruthless of the Somali warlords," Donovan said. "He was educated in Europe and was brutal toward anyone who opposed him. He starved the people as a form of punishment as his whole country stood in fear of him so much so that he went ahead and declared himself as the 'President.'"

Gordon, Shughart and other members of his Delta Force team would be sent to Mogadishu, Somalia to become part of "Task Force Ranger". Task Force Ranger would be a combination of various military elite units from all branches; the Army, Air Force, Navy, and Marines. This unit came about as Somali warlord Mohamed Farrah Aidid's militia had employed a remote controlled bomb against an American humvee, killing four soldiers inside. Aidid would not stop there as two weeks later his soldiers used the same tactic and enjoyed seven more American soldiers. President Bill Clinton then decided to send in an elite task force which was comprised of over 400 U.S. Army rangers and Delta Force members.

They would go to Mogadishu and take down Aidid.

"The number of elite soldiers that Clinton sent was astonishing," Donovan said. "And he did so without proper air support. He was too rash to realize that what was about to happen would be the deadliest closed-arms conflict the United States military would face since the Vietnam War."

The first assignment for Gary and Randy would be to be a part of Operation Gothic Serpent.

Gary would be assigned as the team leader as their mission was to take down a pair of lieutenants to Aidid.

On October 3rd, 1993, special forces were informed that the lieutenants were at a home in the "Black Sea" neighborhood of Mogadishu. The joint-forces would send over 19 aircraft, 12 vehicles and over 160 soldiers to arrest them.

"The raid was supposed to last less than thirty minutes," Donovan said. "But when an American Black Hawk helicopter was shot down, everything went south."

The two Aidid lieutenants were arrested relatively fast by the joint-forces. They were taken into the convoy of ground vehicles but a group of armed Aidid militia members and civilians attacked the group. One American soldier, Dominick Pilla, was killed during the skirmish.

"The arresting convoy didn't realize that how many other people were with Aidid's lieutenants," Donovan said. "They were transporting the prisoners then started to take fire. Then all hell broke loose."

One of the American Black Hawk helicopters, Super Six one, was shot down by a Somalian using a rocket-propelled grenade.

A Combat Search and Rescue team were sent to the crash site to assist any survivors. But a second Black Hawk helicopter, Super Six Four, was shot down by another rocket-propelled grenade. The Combat Search and Rescue team were already engaged in the first crash site and could not help the crew of the second crash. They were exchanging fire with Aidid's soldiers and had their hands full.

One of the pilots inside was Michael Durant.

"There is evidence that suggests (al-Qaeda) was involved in Somalia," Durant said. "I think there is more than some. There is quite a bit of evidence that leads to that. It is logical because al-Qaeda existed at the time (1993) we know now. We know that they've always been gunning for us if you will, this was an opportunity for them to help another organization that was fighting against the U.S. What we forget is that al-Qaeda really got all of their tactical training in Afghanistan fighting the Soviets. So a lot of what they knew, we taught them. We taught them how to shoot down Russian helicopters. So they took those skills and brought them to Somalia is the theory and once they came on the scene we started losing helicopters. We hadn't lost any for the whole time we were there and then suddenly in a period of two weeks we lost seven helicopters."

Durant's copter crashed violently, severely injuring the occupants. Durant's right femur had snapped and he suffered a cracked vertebrae plus the impact of the crash knocked him unconscious. The three other occupants in the copter were alive as well but some had suffered injuries even more severe than Durant.

No one could move.

Captain Jim Yacone, one of the pilots of Super Six-Two, called in for permission to go to the ground to save whoever remained from the wreckage. But Lieutenant Colonel Tom

Matthews, the Air Mission Commander did not want to risk losing more American soldiers.

"Wait," Matthews said. "We don't even know if anyone's alive yet."

The pilots of Super Six-Two then made a pass over the crash site. They spotted Durant who was struggling to free himself from the wreckage that had collapsed on his legs. Chief Warrant Officer Ray Frank could also be seen moving. There was also movement in the rear of the helicopter which made the pilots think that one or both of the gunners were still alive.

"Survivors present," Yacone radioed to mission command.

"Hold on," Matthews said.

Gordon and Shughart continued to shoot down Skinnies who were moving in on the wreckage.

"Things are getting bad now guys," Yacone screamed over the helicopter's engine and the machine gun blasts. "The second convoy is taking intensive fire, and it doesn't sound like it's gonna make the crash site. Mike (his co-pilot) and I have ID'd a field about twenty-five to fifty yards away from where they're down. There are lots of shacks and shanties in between. Once you get there, you could either hunker down and wait for the vehicles, or try to get the wounded to an open area, where we could come back in and get you."

"Drop us down," Gordon said.

The duo landed on the ground and battled their way to the crash site. They ran and shot their way to the helicopter site, going through the shanty town as per their Delta Force training.

"Durant would later say that there was about a ten minute down time after the helicopter was shot down," Donovan said. "The Somalis scrambled to get out of the way and probably feared the copter would explode. The explosion was huge and violent, scaring the shit out of the Skinnies."

Gary and Randy would make it to the wreckage but knew they only had minutes before the Somali soldiers converged, eager to capture, humiliate and kill any American soldier.

"This was an act of incredible heroism," Donovan said. "Both Gary and Randy had enough experience to know that the likelihood of them making it out alive was slim and none. Yet they offered their assistance without any hesitation. This offering came not once but they insisted upon it three times before mission command finally relented. They couldn't just not do anything and watch as their fellow soldier was mauled by a group of Skinnies. They made the decision of death before dishonor."

Gordon and Shughart reached the Super Six Four helicopter, extracting the pilot, Chief Warrant Officer Mike Durant, Bill Cleveland, Tommy Field and Ray Frank. The soldiers then established

defensive positions on the ground, taking down numerous Somali soldiers in the process.

Shughart and Gordon came upon the crash site and assisted Durant first. "They raised me up gently as if handling an ostrich egg," Durant said.

The two men carried the pilot to the right of the chopper, propping his back against the wreckage. Then they gave him his MP-5 machine gun and a spare magazine to help ward off the Skinnies.

"Durant would later say that he had a good view of what was going on on that side of the helicopter," Donovan said. "He could shoot down enemy soldiers coming from that direction. But he worried about the other side of the helicopter as there was a much larger field."

With the rescue unfinished, Gary and Randy entered the rear of the copter where they lifted Bill Cleveland out of the wreckage. Cleveland was semi-conscious and in great pain, his pant legs covered in blood. Gordon and Shughart then went to help Ray Frank and Tommy Field.

"They were like Batman and Robin," Durant said. "Only much better. They just walked up to my aircraft like they were out for a stroll in the park."

They returned back to Durant, indicating that they were looking for a place with enough expanse so that a chopper could land and get them out of there.

"Randy and Gary knew what they were doing," Durant said. "They were calm and deliberate, talking to each other like a couple of surveyors planning a new parking lot, but I knew they were frustrated."

The situation looked hopeless. The ground forces would not arrive in time. The Somali horde would be upon them at any minute.

They would have to locate another place to land a helicopter and even if they did they would have to move four seriously wounded men while under enemy fire.

Then the heard the voices.

Angry Somali voices drawing near, behind a tin wall.

Durant quickly fired through the wall and the voices went silent.

More enemy soldiers arrived, however, and the two Delta snipers found themselves surrounded. Running out of ammo, Gordon moved to the left side of the helicopter, fighting off the horde until he got shot himself.

"Damn, I'm hit," Durant would hear Gordon say.

"It wasn't so much what he said but how he said it," Durant said. "He almost sounded irritated, like this was just going to make things harder for him. It wasn't a scream or a plea, just a statement of fact, like someone who'd nicked himself with a vegetable knife."

With his rescuer now injured, Durant quickly realized how dire the situation had become. Gordon and Shughart were the only hope of the crew.

Gordon had been shot in the head and spleen, directly beneath his body armor.

"There was some controversy as to who got killed first," Donovan said. "Shughart or Gordon. Initially, people believed that Randy was killed first but it was most likely

Gary. Randy had retrieved Gary's gun and gave it to Durant. It is unlikely that Gary would have relinquished his weapon to anyone had he been able to use it."

Shughart radioed about to one of the Little Bird helicopters. He told them that he would make it to an open field.

But time was running out.

Shughart blazed away with his rifle, mowing down Somali soldiers like insects. But more ants kept popping out of the hill. The amount of gunfire he began to receive increased as the minutes progressed.

Shughart battled valiantly until he became overwhelmed as the soldiers of the Somali National Alliance had come on the scene and organized the Skinnies into a more coordinated attack.

"The Somalis regrouped then attacked," Donovan said. "They knew that the Americans were outnumbered and wounded."

Durant would hear the shooting go on for another minute until the gunfire ceased.

Fifteen minutes after his friend Gordon was killed, Shughart succumbed to enemy fire.

Gordon and Shughart had killed twenty-five Somalis total and wounded much more.

Durant then stood alone against the growing Somali horde. Nightmarish thoughts entered his mind of stories he had heard about the savagery of the Skinnies. Ripping bodies apart, chopping off heads and playing soccer with the skull.

Durant killed two of the Somali soldiers before being captured and beaten. The Skinnies broke his nose and fractured his eye-socket. But he was spared execution by a militia chief who saw him as a bargaining chip.

Aidid's supporters then took the body of Bill Cleveland and stripped him naked. They then dragged his body throughout the streets of Mogadishu. This iconic and sadistic imagery made its way to the American media and shocked the viewing public.

"The Somali people desecrated an American soldier's corpse," Donovan said. "And President Clinton's response was to pull out of the region and abandon his pursuit of Aidid. This did not sit well with a lot of members of the United States military as he denied the troops the use of gunship coverage during the battle. There was over two billion dollars spent and no serviceable government in Somalia."

Osama Bin Laden would later cite Clinton's pullout as proof that American had lost its will.

"One American was dragged through the streets of Mogadishu you left," Bin Laden said. "The extent of your impotence and weaknesses became very clear."

MEDAL OF HONOR

On May 23rd, 1994, both Gordon and Shughart would receive the Medal of Honor posthumously. They would become the first Medal of Honor recipients since the

Vietnam War. The medals were presented by Bill Clinton to their wives Carmen Gordon and Stephanie Shughart in a White House ceremony.

Randall's father, Herbert would attend the Medal of Honor presentation ceremony. But Herbert would refuse to shake hands with President Bill Clinton as he blamed him for the death of his son.

"You are not fit to be president of the United States," Herbert told Clinton. "The blame for my son's death rests with the White House and with you. You are not fit to command."

Herbert proceeded to rip into Clinton and according to witnesses, the exchange became a "highly charged emotional moment." Clinton then tried to explain to Shughart's father why the death of his son was not his fault. Herbert stood his ground, knowing that the troops had been refused the proper equipment and support to complete the mission.

Herbert Shughart would later be upset that these details were released to the public. But he never denied that the heated conversation took place and lasted over fifteen minutes.

"That's a pretty fair statement (of what happened)," Herbert Shughart recalled. "I was very upset that the White House aides leaked the details of what was supposed to be a private meeting. We were told that President Clinton wanted to meet my family in private. What I want to know is what part of private doesn't he understand. This story (the argument) didn't come from me. It came from somebody working for him."

"The medal doesn't help anything," said Lois Shughart, Randall's mother. "Other than that we are grateful that Randy will be remembered in such an honorable way."

"Clinton's foreign policies were head scratchers," Donovan said. "By pulling out of the region, he left a huge vacuum for al-Qaeda and other radical Muslim forces to take power. He waffled and made America look as if it would not fight back once things got tough. Since then, numerous factions have risen and grown in strength. But if Mogadishu would occur today, we would have effective use of drones and be able to determine just how many people were in that house with the two lieutenants. But for that skirmish going south, Black Hawk Down would have never occurred."

NAVY SHIPS AND SCHOOLS

Gordon would have a roll-on/roll-off ship named after him, the USNS Gordon on July 4th, 1996. This would be a ship that would be converted from a commercial container vessel to a sealift ship operated by the U.S. Navy's Military Sealift Command.

Shughart would also have a roll-on/roll-off ship named after him. The USNS Shughart was christened in 1997 at the National Steel and Shipbuilding Company in San Diego, California.

Gordon Elementary School opened in Linden Oaks, North Carolina in January of 2009 and was named in honor of Gary Gordon. The school is in close proximity to Fort

Brag where Gordon was stationed before being sent to Somalia. At the Joint Readiness Training Center in Louisiana, the mock city is named Shughart-Gordon.

AFTERMATH

Both Gordon and Shughart were portrayed in the 2001 film, Black Hawk Down.

Carmen Gordon avoids all media portrayals of her husband's final days. She didn't watch the film adaptation but her son Ian did as he wanted to connect somehow with what his father felt on that day.

To this day, the Gordon family has not found complete closure.

"Because our kids were so young when he died and because it was a closed casket. It doesn't feel like he's there (Gordon's grave site). It felt like it was just a gray, steel casket at his funeral. We feel closer to photos, videos, and good memories of Gary than we do visiting the grave site. Seeing his grave just brings back bad, horrible memories."

Stephanie Shughart would later write a heartfelt letter to Michael Durant thanking him for his bravery.

"It is one of the most touching letters I've ever read," Donovan said. "She thanks Durant for never giving up. For surviving so that he could tell the story of how Shughart died while trying to save another man. She gives him permission to go on, live life and be happy."

Gary Gordon and Randy Shughart lived by a creed. A creed that was written across the movie posters for Black Hawk Down.

"Leave no man behind."

"It takes a remarkable person," Stephanie Shughart said. "Not just to say and memorize a creed, but to live by a creed."

Randy Shughart and Gary Gordon were those types of remarkable men.

BOB KALSU : COUNTRY OVER FOOTBALL

115

DEREK HURLEY

James Robert "Bob" Kalsu – He Chose Country Over Football

James Robert "Bob" Kalsu was an esteemed member of the United States military. A veteran of the Vietnam War, he made the ultimate sacrifice of giving his life for his country. While most used their celebrity status and wealth to avoid going to war, Kalsu, an offensive lineman in the National Football League, chose to commit to active duty. A Second Lieutenant in the United States Army, he served from 1969-1970. Tragically, only eight months after joining the fight, Kalsu was killed in A-Shau Valley, Vietnam. In honor of his service, Kalsu's name has become a permanent part of the Vietnam Veterans Memorial Wall in Washington, D.C.

Kalsu's Rearing, Character and Faith

Born in 1945, Kalsu was the only child of Frank and Leah Kalsu. His parents were middle-class and raised him in Del City, a small town outside of Oklahoma City. Kalsu's family took great pride in their Czechoslovakian heritage. They would also raise young Bob to be a committed Catholic and man of faith. As a part of that faith, Kalsu learned to be true to his word and to think of others above himself. These teachings would influence him in both his football and military career, and would lead him to make the choice to serve in Vietnam.

Kalsu in High School

At a young age, Kalsu became interested in all types of sports. But aspiring to be like his Uncle Charles (an All-American and college basketball star), he focused mainly on basketball and football. Kalsu's father Frank had also aspired to be an athlete but didn't have the talent. Early on however, Frank saw the talent in his son and not only encouraged, but pushed him to work and train hard. Consequently, young Bob Kalsu became a remarkable athlete. While attending Del City High School, along with sports, Kalsu served as a newspaper reporter.

Playing on the varsity football team, Kalsu became an exceptional player. He was an offensive lineman but the coach would often use him to both kick and punt. Soon the word got around about his skills and abilities resulting in many college recruiters coming to watch Kalsu play. This included the pride of Oklahoma, the University of Oklahoma Sooners where his Uncle Charles had once excelled on the basketball team.

Outside of school sports, Bob Kalsu also enjoyed bowling, golf and playing board games.

Years as an Oklahoma Sooner

Although Kalsu had offers from numerous colleges, desiring to stay close to home and follow family tradition, Kalsu accepted a football scholarship from the University of Oklahoma Sooners. He also wanted very much to play for Bud Wilkinson, a coach known for his candor, assertiveness and powerful presence in the football world. Nevertheless, Kalsu would not get this opportunity as Wilkinson retired from the University of Oklahoma just before his freshman season. Instead, Chuck Fairbanks coached and helped Kalsu become a championship player during his college career.

As a Sooner, Kalsu thrived on the gridiron. He was an offensive lineman known for his powerful tackles and quick feet. An All-American, he was a hard worker and both a respected and commanding team leader. In fact, Kalsu played a crucial role on the team that defeated Tennessee in the 1967 Orange Bowl.

He also succeeded in the classroom, especially in the Reserve Officers Training Corp (ROTC) program. In 1968, Kalsu graduated with a Bachelor's Degree from the University of Oklahoma and also became a commissioned officer in the United States Army.

Kalsu Gets Married

In the second semester of his senior year of college, Bob married his bride Jan after a long courtship. Jan was the daughter of a local physician and came from a very large family. Bob having been an only child, quickly gained lots of siblings which was a joy to him. By graduation, Jan was already pregnant with their first child.

Drafted by the Buffalo Bills

Also in his senior year of college, Kalsu's dreams of playing professional football would come true. In the eighth round of the 1968 NFL draft, the Buffalo Bills selected Kalsu as one of their team picks. Both the Dallas Cowboys and Denver Broncos had also shown interest and strongly considered him, but would shy away concerned about his military commitment.

In his first and only season of the NFL, Kalsu would have the chance to play in all 14 games and start in 8. As a Buffalo Bill, Kalsu excelled as a rookie; so much so, he was selected "Rookie of the Year".

Kalsu Chooses Country Over Football and Goes to Vietnam

Having become a commissioned officer upon graduation from the University of Oklahoma, Kalsu had a commitment to the United States Army. A successful player in the NFL, Kalsu could have gone to the Bills' front office to seek help in getting out of his orders to Vietnam. He could have also requested transfer to a reserve unit to avoid active duty as many others had done. But despite the urging of his coaches, family and friends, Kalsu would do the opposite and accepted his orders as passed down. When asked why, he said he felt it was his duty to serve in the war. He also stated that he took his commission serious and believed going was part of his obligation as a military officer.

Kalsu in Vietnam

As a Second Lieutenant in the United States Army, Kalsu was part of the 101st Airborne Division. His subordinates described him as a fair and inspirational leader who always led by example. Although he didn't talk much about his professional athlete status while in Vietnam, Kalsu used many of the skills he learned as a football player to lead his platoon.

Although he was a military officer, Kalsu would often help with menial tasks, a trait that earned him the loyalty and admiration of his men. One of those men was David Johnson, a young African-American from a small town in Arkansas. In the 101st Airborne Division, many considered Kalsu and Johnson best friends. Perhaps they bonded over their love for sports and family, or maybe it was their faith. No matter the reason, their relationship was genuine and built upon trust, love and respect.

In the midst of the Vietnam War, Kalsu exhibited a great sense of humor and relaxed attitude. He was often the prankster in his unit, and loved to play games (although he would cheat whenever he could). Forever the athlete, because he planned to return to his football career after the war, Kalsu continued to train while in Vietnam. He would run up hills carrying sacks and ammunition to keep his body in condition.

A Fallen Hero – Kalsu Dies in Action

In the summer of 1970, the 101st Division engaged in an intense, near month long battle with the North Vietnamese Army on the hilltop of Ripcord. Their mission was to destroy the supply base for the Viet Cong leaving them with inadequate equipment, food and other necessities thus weakening their power. Unlike other officers, in this battle, Kalsu would get right in the trenches with his men. He didn't seek safety giving orders from his bunker like many officers did, but instead he moved around checking on his men to make sure they were okay.

On July 21, 1970, as Kalsu always did, he was out and about in the midst of the fire fight giving orders and seeing about his team. Although he'd been able to avoid injury thus far, that day he would meet his fate. Just steps away from his bunker, he was hit with a mortar shell and killed instantly. Being they were atop a small mountain with men shoulder to shoulder, this blast resulted in many casualties and fatalities. One of those fatally wounded was James Robert "Bob" Kalsu. Nearby and just steps away from the body of Kalsu they'd also find his buddy and best friend, David Johnson. Kalsu was only 25 years old when he perished.

Earlier on that same day, Kalsu had received a letter from his wife giving him an update on her pregnancy. He learned from that letter that she would give birth in the next couple of days. Extremely excited, Kalsu looked forward to being a dad again and had high hopes that she would have a boy. Unfortunately, after his death, this story would become totally distorted. Instead of the truth that Kalsu received a letter much earlier in the day, some say he was killed while running to the helicopter anxious to hear news about the birth of his baby. This was such a prevalent rumor, even Kalsu's family believed it for a while. Later however, one of Kalsu's comrades would come forth with the truth which gave his family more peace.

Laid to Rest

Along with his wife, children and parents, Kalsu, Sr. left behind numerous aunts, uncles, nieces, nephews, in-laws and friends to grieve his death. At the request of the family, the military shipped Kalsu, Sr.'s body home for burial. Honoring their heritage and family tradition, Czechoslovakian National Cemetery in Oklahoma City was the venue for the funeral service. Attended by many local friends, fellow servicemen and teammates including some from the Buffalo Bills, it was an emotional gathering. Kalsu's burial plot is located in the center of that same cemetery in a special place designated for veterans. He is the most famous person buried in this quiet and secluded graveyard.

The Family Robert "Bob" Kalsu, Sr. Left Behind

When deployed to Vietnam, Bob's daughter Jill was less than a year old and Jan was also expecting their second child. Jan and Jill would see Bob for the last time when he took leave from Vietnam to Hawaii for one week. During that week, they enjoyed spending time together as a family and seeing the island sites. When leaving, Bob made Jan promise to take care of herself and the baby. She too told Bob to stay safe and out of harm's way.

A couple of days after Kalsu's death, Jan would give birth to a little boy. She and Bob's mom knew he would be ecstatic about having a son. However, they did not yet know that Kalsu, Sr. was already dead. It would be in the hospital just hours after giving birth that they'd receive a visit from the military officer who delivered the tragic news. Consequently, Jan decided to name her son Robert Kalsu, Jr. in honor of his dad.

Jan was only 22 years of age when she became a single parent to Jill and Robert, Jr. Desiring to continue to be a stay-at-home mom, she struggled financially but was able to rear her children with the help of family, especially her in-laws. During their childhood, Robert, Jr. and Jill's grandfather Frank (Bob's dad) played the role of father. Being a strong paternal figure, he would attend their sporting events, school plays and choir concerts. He also taught them to have the same care for people, to be honest and walk in integrity just as he had instructed their father, his son. But while they were still in their young teens, Frank would pass away after a lengthy battle with cancer. This was a huge blow to the children. Their grandmother, Leah, however lived into her early 80's. The entire family, Frank, Leah and Bob, Sr. are all buried, (although not beside each other) in the Czech National Cemetery.

Although Jill had the chance to know her father, she was so young that she barely recalls anything about him. Of course Robert, Jr. never even had the chance to meet their father. Still, they have come to know him through the many friends and fellow soldiers their dad left behind. Kalsu, Sr. also left a number of voice messages for them to listen to along with many photographs from his college and professional football days.

Bob Kalsu, Sr's widow has since remarried, but never had any more children. She continues to represent her first husband at events throughout the community and in the state of Oklahoma. Her new husband is also very supportive and often travels along with her. Bob Kalsu, Jr. and Jill Kalsu-Homing are both proud of their dad's legacy and are instilling what they believe to be his values in their children. Kalsu, Jr. who is now an attorney in Oklahoma often stands in for the family at military and sporting events held in honor of his dad. Although he enjoys hearing tributes to his father, he says these appearances can be emotionally draining for him.

Inducted into the Pro Football Hall of Fame

The Pro Football Hall of Fame, located in Canton, Ohio, celebrates the history of professional football and pays tributes to many of its top players. This gallery has a special exhibit dedicated to football players who were also American heroes. Bob Kalsu, Sr. is one of the players honored here with a plaque given to the museum from the Buffalo Bills. Unveiled and dedicated at a ceremony in 1978, this plaque tells the story of Kalsu's life including his football career and the sacrifice he made at Ripcord.

NFL Film About Bob Kalsu, Sr.

In 1999, Kalsu became the star of an episode of <u>NFL Films Presents</u>. This short documentary entitled <u>Remembering Bob </u>Kalsu tells the story of his life from childhood until death. It includes interviews with his former Buffalo Bills roommate, fellow servicemen and Bob's wife Jan. Moving and inspiring, it features a voice recording of Kalsu leaving an endearing message for his wife, daughter and unborn son. An outstanding piece of work, it was later nominated for and received an Emmy Award.

The Buffalo Bills Pay Tribute

The Buffalo Bills front office, coaches and players will never forget the sacrifice Bob Kalsu, Sr. made in Vietnam. Former teammates and current players not only pay tribute to him annually at their Salute to Service game, but the team has also honored him with a place on the Buffalo Bills' Wall of Fame at New Era Field. A special day was set aside and a formal ceremony held to unveil the display to the public. Kalsu's family attended the ceremony and many of his teammates participated in the dedication. The plaque which now hangs in Ralph Wilson Stadium reads as follows: "No one will ever know how great a football player Bob might have been, but we do know how great a man he was to give up his life for his country."

Seeking to continue Kalsu's legacy of putting others above oneself, the Buffalo Bills' Booster Club gives away a $1,000 scholarship each year to a senior from Oklahoma. Recipients are selected by committee based upon scholarship along with volunteerism and involvement in sports and other school activities.

Display at the Naval & Military Park

Additionally, the Buffalo community has paid homage to Kalsu with an exhibit located in the Naval & Military Park. This display includes many of his personal items on loan from his family along with his Buffalo Bill's helmet.

The Oklahoma Vietnam Veterans Memorial Association

Established in the late 1990's, the Oklahoma Vietnam Veterans Memorial Association provides scholarships to students annually in the names of Bob Kalsu, Sr. and Riley Pitts (another military officer from Oklahoma who died in Vietnam). Funded via donations, each year the association hosts a banquet to raise more money to endow the program. The Bob Kalsu, Sr. Scholarship awards $1500 to a deserving student and is renewable for four years.

Other Memorials Honoring Bob Kalsu, Sr.

As the plaque on the Buffalo Bills Wall of Fame states, we will never know the achievements Kalsu could have made in the game of football. Nonetheless, we do know that he was an unselfish man who chose commitment to country over money and fame. Because of this, his name deserves honor and a place in United States history. Instead, after his funeral, his name went into obscurity along with that of many other fallen Vietnam Vets. Kalsu's family also opted to grieve in private and did not welcome a lot of media attention. This may have also delayed him receiving the recognition he was due.

Although Kalsu's story didn't get much public attention immediately following the war, he would go from anonymity to fame in 2001 when <u>Sports Illustrated</u> made Bob Kalsu, Sr. the cover athlete for one of their summer issues. Along with a cover photo, there was a lengthy article about his life as an athlete and serviceman inside the magazine. This article served to introduce Kalsu to a new generation and sparked added interest in this American hero.

The University of Oklahoma, namely its athletic department, has received the most criticism for not acknowledging Kalsu, Sr. as a fallen soldier. There is however a tribute to Kalsu noting his football stats and accomplishments placed outside of the Jack Santee Lounge of Oklahoma's Memorial Stadium. Oklahoma has also acknowledged Kalsu with an athletic scholarship named for him and two other Sooners. Known as the Benien, Kalsu and Henderson scholarship, this scholarship is awarded to a graduate student who has lettered at the University of Oklahoma in a varsity sport. The athletic department, some say, has failed however to honor him in terms of his military service. Outside of the athletic department, the alumni of the ROTC program has developed the Bob Kalsu Character Award, a $500 scholarship awarded to a student who shows themselves to be a leader with integrity and character like that of Bob Kalsu, Sr.

Other tributes to Bob Kalsu, Sr. include the renaming of the Del City High School Football Stadium now known as the Robert Kalsu Stadium. Additionally, the Army's Fort Campbell Replacement Company in Kentucky also bears his name. Lastly, in 2015, Congress voted to rename the Del City Post Office the James Robert Kalsu Post Office. Kalsu's family along with Congressman Steve Russell of Oklahoma's 5th Congressional District attended a ceremony and reception later in 2015 to commemorate the occasion.

AARON BANK:

THE FATHER OF THE GREEN BERETS

125

STEVE GOLDMAN

Aaron Bank was born November 23rd, 1902 in New York City to Russian immigrants. He was employed as the primary life guard at an upscale resort in Biarritz, located on the Bay of Biscayne. His mother was a language teacher and tutored Bank on how to speak French, German and Spanish which enabled him to become a popular fixture at the resort. During the winter, Bank would travel to the Bahamas and work as a lifeguard there.

Throughout Bank's travels and in conversations he had in Europe, he had a sixth sense that a war was coming. He noted that in Germany, men were marching around with shovels like rifles on their shoulders. There were torchlight parades and war mongering songs. Bank saw the writing on the wall and enlisted in 1939, getting a commission from Officer Candidate School.

Entering the U.S. Army at the advanced age of thirty-seven, he was initially thought to be "too old" for military duty. His swimming and physical conditioning, however, proved to be a tough offer to refuse so Bank was accepted into the Office of Strategic Services (OSS) during World War II.

"There was an 'old man's registration' for the draft," military historian Chuck Walsh said. "Around 1942, the military was sending out draft cards to men as old as forty-five. So, in hindsight, Bank should not have been discriminated against because of his age especially when you take into consideration his tremendous physical conditioning."

The OSS did both both espionage operations (SI Branch) and special operations (SO Branch), for sabotage and guerrilla warfare. Bank was sent to the SO Branch initially.

"Officers who could speak a foreign language were invited to volunteer," Bank said. "Actually, that was a godsend. In early 1943, I was a tactical training officer for a railroad battalion at Camp Polk, La.—a real hellhole. I was considered too old for combat in the infantry, my original branch. The OSS was my chance to get into the war, and I jumped at it"

COUNTRY CLUB TRAINING?

Bank began training for the OSS at the Congressional Country Club in Washington D.C.

The surroundings were "plush" and not the rugged terrain you would expect for commando training. The OSS trained on the golf course and along the Potomac river. Later he was sent to England for additional training which increased in intensity. Bank now learned at the feet of men who had fought with guerrillas in Yugoslavia, Greece and France.

Bank became an expert in communications, demolitions, weapons, hand-to-hand combat, subversion, sabotage and guerrilla warfare. The training for these skill sets took place between different manor houses in Scotland and England, as Bank traveled from one different training compound to the next.

Bank would find parachute training to be the most fear-inducing as they made him jump from a hot air balloon. Because there was no propeller blast from an airplane, a soldier would fall about two-hundred feet before the parachute opened. They were also given no reserve parachutes.

THE JEDBURGH TEAM

On July 31, 1944, at the advanced military age of 42, he led the Jedburgh Team as they parachuted into France and teamed up with the French Resistance.

Initially, the special operations teams were called "Jedburghs". The name was taken from a town in Scotland where Scots, during their wars with England, engaged in guerrilla warfare. These Jedburghs would consist of two officers and a radio operator. The teams were self-selected with the thinking being that "compatible individuals would form their own natural groups."

The majority of the Jedburghs were represented by soldiers who came from countries that were occupied by Germany (France, Belgium, Netherlands). General Charles de Gaulle, however, ordered that any team going into France would have to have a French officer. French soldiers were highly sought after for this position and Bank found himself partnered up with two Frenchmen.

"We had an American radio operator initially, but the French officer, Henri, was concerned that if something happened to me he would not be able to communicate effectively with an American," Bank said. "So Jean [the French never revealed their surnames for security reasons] became our radio operator. I'm still in touch with the American radio operator, Bill Thompson, who went on to earn a Croix de Guerre with another team."

"The Jeds were ahead of their time when it came to secret codes and clandestine operations," Walsh said. "They used pieces of cloth that had five hundred phrases that they would use in radio traffic replaced with four letter codes. This would be a kind of messaging short-hand, if you will, and allowed them to encrypt their messages."

LIVING WITH PIGS

There was some friction between some of the French and British operatives for a little while but things cooled off when they confronted their common enemy. Bank was shipped to Algiers where he was stationed with French colonial troops. He found the ground littered with soiled toilet paper as there was no outhouse and the soldiers would defecate whenever the need arose. It made for an unsanitary environment and Bank came down with a fever along with many other Americans.

He went to a hospital for treatment but was then visited by his team member, Henri, who told him they would be leaving for France that night. Bank then sneaked past the MP's guarding the hospital gate, heading off to World War II in his pajamas.

OPERATION OVERLORD

That July of 1944, Bank parachuted into France as part of Operation Overlord, armed nothing but a pocketful of money. The plane dropped canisters of medical supplies, explosives, bullets and

Sten guns. There would be a total of 93 different Jeds inserted in over fifty French towns between June and December of 1944. The used first names like "Hugh" or the names of medicines like "Novacaine" for code names to throw off German intelligence.

Bank parachuted in at night and meet a member of the reception committee from the local resistance. Bank was picked up in a truck that was powered by a charcoal boiler as the Germans had taken control of all the gasoline.

Despite the mission being Top Secret, Bank's arrival with his team members seem to be known by all involved.

The villagers lined the streets as the commandos made their way through the town cheering them on, not exactly keeping their arrival secret.

Bank did not want the attention. He wanted to get organized, train and wait for the invasion. He went from camp to camp, training the different guerrilla leaders who would then pass on the training to their men. Most of the trainees were experienced French soldiers but Bank still had to correct them to not stay in one place for too long. He also noticed that the camps were too close together. This would allow the Germans to find out where a food shortage was and determine the whereabouts of the camp as food was being rationed in France. Bank advised to keep the camps moving and spread apart but close enough that they could be called upon if necessary.

ADDITIONAL PROBLEMS

"One problem was medical support," Bank said. "It is hard to recruit a guerrilla if he thinks he might suffer a minor wound and then be left behind—perhaps to be tortured, certainly to be killed, by the Germans. We enlisted a French doctor to operate an aid station in a barn and set up a system to move serious cases to hospitals in smaller towns that were relatively safe. Another problem was ammunition. We had all sorts of weapons—American, British, French, German. Many of them used bullets that were similar but not exactly the same."

There were other problems trying to separate different types of ammunition. On one occasion, Bank's unit had fired upon a truck convoy but had to retreat when the machine gunner had bullets of two different calibers in the belt. The wrong bullet was fed into the chamber and the gun jammed. During another fire fight, Bank's squad hit a convoy with mortar fire but the explosives did not detonate. Instead, smoke covered the enemy and they could not see what the Germans were doing. They once again had to withdraw with Bank telling the French forces to throw away the smoke rounds.

The Frenchmen, however, refused Bank's advice. "The French never throw anything away," Bank would later say.

CHAIN OF COMMAND

"The guerrillas had their own leaders," Bank said. "If we had tried to take over their operation, we would have been lucky to get out alive. Our job was to help them plan and keep them supplied. But they knew we were there to help them, so they usually did as we advised. And make no mistake about it, they were very courageous. You didn't have to kick them in the ass to make them fight."

The Germans would retaliate in terroristic fashion to the guerrilla ambushes. If the attack occurred too close to a town, the Germans would round up all of the men and boys in the village and execute them as if they were co-conspirators. Bank's squad tried their hardest to stage the ambushes between the towns so the Germans would not know which town would be "responsible." In the end, however, the Nazis would end up taking men and boys from both towns, invariably holding them hostage or executing them.

The mayors of some of the towns demanded that the guerillas move somewhere else, fearing German retaliation. Henri and the rest of the guerrilla leaders did not consent, however. They would inform the town leaders that the price of freedom was high and people would be sacrificed.

With limited supplies, the guerrilla groups would compete for rations and equipments. Bank belonged to the Forces Françaises de l'Interieur [FFI], the nationalists. The Franc-Tireurs Partisans [FTP], were Communists in the same region. The FTP stole some of the FFI's resupply drops.

OPERATION DRAGOON

Bank and the rest of the 3,000 guerillas went all out on the night of August 14, 1944, the day before the Allied forces landed in southern France. Between Marseille and Lyon, the dozens of guerrilla bands that Bank had trained were keeping numerous German divisions occupied. They then prevented the Germans from retreating into the mountains and kept them pinned down in the Rhône Valley, where the Air Force took over as the guerrilla units were able to cut off the Nazi retreat to the north.

All told the guerrillas killed about 1,000 German soldiers. Some of the guerrilla units didn't always want to take prisoners but Bank convinced them otherwise, locking up the Nazi soldiers in town jails throughout his sector.

LIBERATION

The French were absolutely jubilant after southern France was liberated.

"We had ambush sites outside of town," Bank said, recalling when he was stationed at a German escape route. "When word came that the Germans were coming, everything shut down. All the shops were closed, windows were shuttered, and there was no one on the street. When word came that the Germans had been driven back, the cafes opened, wine flowed, people crowded into the streets, and the fireman's band played. Then word would come of another German column approaching, and the town would shut down again. This was repeated over and over again during the next three or four days until advanced elements of the U.S. Seventh Army arrived."

Bank and the guerillas cleaned up the towns, searching for hiding German soldiers. They went from house to house, finding a Nazi holed up here and there. The guerrilla teams would suffer the most casualties during this time. Both the FFI and the FTP journeyed through the villages, cleaning them up and leaving a local government in power. But if the FTP got there first,they would set up a Communist controlled administration.

Bank's FFI group did not want that too happen so they hurried through town after town.

On only one occasion, however, did the FFI and FTP clash.

The FTP had beaten Bank's FFI to Nîmes, removing the mayor and other city officials out of city hall. A group of French citizens came to Bank and asked for help. They were informed that the Seventh Army would be arriving soon but the citizens insisted that Bank's team establish order now.

Bank and the FFI then strolled past the FTP roadblocks and into the city, taking positions on rooftops and around the town.

The FFI then informed the Communists they could leave safely if the left immediately.

The FTP then retreated out of the town as the local citizenry showered them with rocks and bottles. Bank then went out to the balcony of the city hall to make a speech. They saw the American flag sewn onto his shoulder sleeve and began to chant 'Vive les Américains!'

The fighting finally ended in September. American and French troops secured the region and the guerillas were absorbed back into the armies of their respective countries.

Bank returned to the OSS headquarters in London.

OPERATION IRON CROSS

Five months later, Bank thought he would be sent to China. The Germans, however, counter attacked and the fighting resumed at the Battle of the Bulge.

In January 1945, Bank was named head of "Operation Iron Cross" which became a plan to capture or kill Adolf Hitler.

The OSS had sought out German POWs who had opposed Hitler and used them to form a special forces unit. These men were given SS uniforms and became highly adept in "raid and snatch" maneuvers.

To their surprise, the OSS was able to recruit many former German Soldiers, predominantly former German Communists, who adamantly opposed Hitler. They also recruited German Jews who had go into exile into the Wehrmacht, posing as Gentiles.

"The Allies feared that top Nazi officials, defended by die-hard Schützstaffel [SS] troops, would flee to the Austrian Alps and make their way to Spain or some other sympathetic neutral country," Bank said. The idea was that I would lead a group of German defectors, military and civilian, and parachute with them into the Inn Valley in Austria. Dressed in German army uniforms, we would conduct subversion, sabotage and guerrilla actions. But our main objective was to capture high-ranking Nazis before they could reach the redoubt in the Alps. When OSS chief Maj. Gen. William Donovan was briefed on the mission, he declared: 'Don't limit it to the capture of Nazi bigwigs. I want Hitler. Tell Bank to get Hitler!'"

DEEP COVER OPERATIVE

A fake identity for Bank was created but he was worried as he could not speak German well enough to be a soldier. He also spoke French with an accent. Instead, he came up with the identity of "Henry Marchand".

Marchand would be a Nazi sympathizer who was born in Martinique. The idea was that the Nazis would have no inkling as to how a citizen from Martinique would sound like. It would also give Bank a pass for not being able to speak German properly. The plan was for him to be a corporal in the ranks and not a German company commander.

RECRUITING THE TEAM

Bank then began recruiting Germans for the Iron Cross mission.

"We started with a German dissident we called Karl," Bank said. "He had lost an arm fighting for the Loyalists in the Spanish Civil War and had fought with the French Resistance. Karl had a list of German prisoners of war [POWs] who might be interested in clandestine work if they were offered early release after the war. Karl then introduced us to Max and Hermann, two other Germans who had fought for the Loyalists in Spain. They would be trained to accompany me into Austria. We suspected they might be Communists, but "Wild Bill" Donovan's philosophy was, 'Use them as long as they kill Nazis.' An OSS team, Karl and I then toured POW camps. We selected more than 125 prisoners. We also recruited, from a holding camp, about 50 German civilians, almost all of whom had fought in the French Resistance."

The recruits were trained for two months on a large manor at St. Germain, west of Paris. They simulated raids, ambushes, hand-to-hand combat.

A lot of physical training and conditioning runs were involved but the recruits soon complained that the exercise program was much tougher than it had been in the German army.

"Bank had trained the men to spend not only weeks but years if necessary, behind enemy lines," Walsh said. "They could be completely independent, knowledgeable about the culture and language of the indigenous population and have the ability to conduct combat maneuvers without assistance of any kind."

Bank screened out individuals who could not meet a standard and chose others to be sergeants and commanders. They didn't do any parachute training but Bank poo-poohed the notion as it wouldn't be the first time that a soldier received only ground school training.

The unit then traveled to Dijon where the OSS had set up headquarters. The men were decked out in German uniforms and waited for the opportunity.

The weather took a turn for the worse, however, and the mission had to be delayed.

A week later Operation Iron Cross was canceled with no official reason.

"I've heard a lot of reasons," Bank said. "That the war was winding down and it was too risky, that the State Department objected to putting more than 100 suspected Communists into Austria at that time, that maybe we had learned of Adolf Hitler's suicide. It's a pity though; in terms of numbers, it would have been the biggest single OSS special operation of the war."

"I never cried in my life, but I damn near cried when they told me it was aborted."

Hitler, it turned out, was in Berlin at the time and the 175 ex-Pows thought he was in his mountain hideaway in Berchtesgaden; he committed suicide in his Berlin bunker on April 30, 1945.

The 101st Airborne and 7th Army divisions were advancing so quickly they were expected to overwhelm whatever forces the Nazis would assemble at Alpine Redoubt. They also realized that Bank's enemy-uniformed volunteers would be seen as the enemy by the allied forces so the project was nixed.

OFF TO CHINA

After Germany's surrender, Bank was sent to China and arrived in Nanking in June of 1945 with a new mission. He was to train a unit of Vietnamese soldiers of the French Army as well as three French officers and lead them in a raid on Japanese headquarters on the Red River near Hanoi.

The mission was daunting, they would have to travel over one-hundred thirty miles through thick jungle in mountainous terrain which was now under Japanese control.

After a month of training, they were ready for the mission to begin.

But like Operation Iron Cross, the mission was delayed then canceled.

The offensive was called off out of fear that Ho Chi Minh and his guerrillas would turn on them instead of continuing to fight the Japanese.

RESCUING OF FRENCH POWS

Two months later, after Bank had been promoted to major, he led a team of special operations and intelligence personnel into Laos.

They searched for hidden POW camps and French refugees, finding fourteen of them.

Bank crossed the Mekong River into Thailand and saw several British Special Air Service teams with guns and ammo. He was not sure who the weapons were for as they crossed back into Laos at Thakhet and on a recon mission they found eight French refugees were captured there by the Japanese. Bank and his men gave them food and medicine. They offered to move them across the river into Thailand but they elected to stay, believing that the French would soon take over.

French Indochina had been split along the 16th parallel for military control. North of the line was the American China Command sector, while the area south of it was under the Southeast Asia Command, which was a British unit with French commandos. The French were attacking north of the line in violation of Allied policy.

Bank asked for instructions and several days passed before he received a reply. He then decided to go back to the Hanoi headquarters of China Command which was several days away.

It was there he met Ho Chi Minh.

"He was a little guy, with a thin wispy beard—and he spoke excellent French," Bank recalled. "But he hated—despised—the French. We rode with him as far as Hue and had quite a discussion. He said that he admired Americans and hoped for an independent Vietnam with political and economic ties to the United States. 'I like you Americans,' he said. 'You are not colonizers like the British and the French. You gave Cuba its freedom, and you are going to do the same with the Philippines.' I thought he was on the level. I knew he was trained in Moscow and was a Communist, but he was a nationalist first."

Bank would inform the OSS of Ho's following among the Vietnamese people and advised that he be allowed to form a coalition government. Bank felt that Ho would win any kind of popular election if Vietnam became a democracy.

President Harry S. Truman felt otherwise, however, seeing Ho as a strident Communist. Ho had joined the party in 1920s in Paris and American policymakers would not see him as an acceptable leader of a coalition government.

There were some French "Vichy" military forces that remained in China and the United States allowed the use of these ancillary forces to block Ho and reinstate Indochina as a French colony.

President Truman and later President Dwight D. Eisenhower would provide financial aid to the French which led to the Indochina War which would then culminate into the Vietnam War.

Bank would return to Thakhet with the attacks in the area intensifying. He met with the French commando leader but realized that he was a British officer in a French uniform. Bank warned him to keep his soldiers out of the American zone.

The Brit-French commander didn't listen and instead intensified their efforts. Bank was then recalled to Nanking and learned that the OSS had been disbanded.

FOUNDING THE SPECIAL FORCES

Bank remained in the Army after the war and began lobbying for the formation of a professional special forces division, which be equivalent to the SO branch of the OSS that he was a part of. Bank, along with Colonel Russel W. Volckmann led the charge in convincing the Army that employing such a unit would be of great benefit.

They described how special forces could be used behind the "Iron Curtain", Eastern European nations controlled by the Soviet Union, where they could oversee local resistance movements.

In 1952, Bank would become the first commander of the Army's first Special Forces unit. This group would be called the 10th Special Forces Group. They used the number ten to confused the Russians who would then suspect that there were nine more units.

"We got the authority in 1952," Bank said. "In the late winter or early spring. It took us a year and a half to convince the Pentagon to authorize a formation of an unconventional warfare unit in the active army. There was a strange coincidence that helped this at the last moment when fate really smiled on us. It was decided to deactivate the Rangers at the that time the European commanders said that they couldn't do, they weren't capable of carrying out a mission organizing guerillas. They weren't language trained and they weren't trained in unconventional warfare. And the Far East commander at the same time had the same opinion so they decided to disband them. And that gave us the spaces, the troops that we needed."

In creating the 10th, Bank had been as flexible with members as he had been with "Iron Cross". He recruited former members of the Devil's Brigade (1st Special Service Force), veterans of the Oss, the Parachute Infantry units and other soldiers who performed guerrilla warfare in the Pacific.

"On the first day of activation there were only ten of us," Bank said. "Myself, a warrant officer and eight enlisted men. That was the beginning of Special Forces in 1952. June of 1952. And you can see how we've grown."

On November 11th, 1953 after an aborted labor riot in communist East Germany, half of the 10th Special Forces Group was sent to Bad Tolz, West Germany. The other half stayed at Fort Bragg and was renamed as the 77th Special Forces Group.

FATHER OF THE GREEN BERETS

Bank would combine all of the lessons and strategies used during World War II to train the elite unit of men. They were trained in foreign languages, techniques of sabotage and stealth, the use of explosives, amphibious warfare, rock climbing, jungle fighting, mountain and snow terrain warfare.

And oh, yes, the men would wear Green Berets.

"The reason (that he's considered the father of the Green Berets) is that Volkmann and I did all the staff work," Bank said. "To gain the approval for such an outfit. But once we had the approval then General McClure gave me command of the unit to go on the field and bring it to reality. That's why I'm called the father."

The Special Forces are still an all volunteer unit and divided into "A teams", having two experts in every specialty.

To be allowed in the group, an individual must survive a grueling training process in which most men fail or quit.

Bank required the same training of the men he recruited for "Operation Iron Cross".

"Special Forces is composed of the same light to the extent that it is really a brotherhood," Bank said. "Of daring, dedicated, highly motivated soldiers. Soldiers who are willing to accept calculated risks. Risks that extend far beyond the normal call of duty. Risks such as jumping and operating behind the lines. But then, one can say, what's so remarkable about that? The conventional airborne and the Marine Recon troops they do the same thing. Yes. They do. But Special Forces go beyond that. They operate deep in enemy territory. Right into the enemy heartland and for indefinite periods. Not two or three days, but for weeks, months or longer and they operate in those areas when required in civilian attire and in enemy uniform and I assure you that that separates the Green Beret trooper from the conventional soldier whether he's Airborne or Straight leg."

RETIREMENT

Bank retired from the Army in 1958 at the age of 56. He would be awarded the Soldier's Medal, Bronze Star with V device, the French Croix de Guerre and the British "mentioned in dispatches" emblem.

THE GREEN BERETS MADE OFFICIAL

Years after his retirement, the green beret could only be worn by soldiers who had earned the Special Forces Tab. In 1956, General Paul D. Adams had initially banned the wearing of the beret even though numerous guerrillas squads were wearing them overseas.

"In 1962, President Kennedy visited Fort Bragg," Bank recalled. "And during a parade there, in his honor, the Special Forces unit there passed by his view wearing berets. And Kennedy liked it. He was also impressed by the Green Berets when he immediately grasped what they could do and he awarded them the Green Beret. Now they had been turned down even in my time I tried to get the Green Beret in the army and the army turned me down. They said there would be no distinctive items of uniform."

STILL VIGILANT

Making his home in San Clemente, California, Bank would start his own personal investigation into the dearth of security at the San Onofre Nuclear Generating Station, a few miles south of San Clemente.

Bank realized that the San Onofre plant was protected by only one security guard armed with a pistol, as if the only concern would be that of theft. Bank saw the potential for disaster here as even one special forces soldier could disable the security guard, infiltrate the plant and destroy it with a set of explosives. The plant would then set off radioactivity into the atmosphere and contaminate thousands of square miles, including Los Angeles.

Bank took the bull by the horn, lobbying bigwigs before testing in front of a closed session of the U.S. Atomic Energy Commission. He presented his findings and warned them of the dangers of a terrorist attack at San Onofre. The AEC dismissed his arguments and did nothing to provide greater security at the facilities.

Bank then teamed with an investigative journalist who then wrote an article exposing the poor security of San Onofre for the Bulletin of the Atomic Scientists in 1974.

This expose would lead to a Congressional investigation and later secret testimony by Bank before a Congressional committee.

This time, Congress forced the AEC and its successor, the Nuclear Regular Commission to enact changes among which include on-site security squads with automatic weapons, remote scram capabilities (to take control of the plant remotely and shut it down in the event of an emergency) and the use of "red teams" to test defenses and eliminate any vulnerabilities.

LIFE BEYOND THE SPECIAL FORCES

Extremely fit and vigorous most of his life, the 5-foot-8, 140-odd-pound Bank swam around the San Clemente pier every day until he was 74. He then took to running 40 minutes a day on the hilly streets near his home.

Bank was also chief of Security on Beach road, a private community of homes along Capistrano Beach. In 1972, at age 70, he began working full time as chief of security at a private oceanfront community in Capistrano Beach, a job he held until he was 85.

Bank would be recognized by President George W. Bush in 2002 on his hundredth birthday. Bush commended him for creating the unconventional warfare programs and techniques that were used in defeating the Taliban.

Bank would die on April 1st, 2004 in Dana Point, California. He was 101 years old.

He is buried at Riverside National Cemetery in Riverside, California.

MELVIN MORRIS : AMERICAN SOLDIER

143

SCOTT FRANK

Medal of Honor Recipient Melvin Morris

Staff Sergeant Melvin Morris is an honored veteran of the Vietnam War. He served almost 30 years in the United States Army and was even part of a Special Forces Group. Brave and excelling at his career in the military, Morris would do two tours of duty in Vietnam before retiring in 1985.

His Early Life

Melvin Morris was born and raised Okmulgee, a close-knit farming community in Oklahoma. He had seven other siblings and was the middle-child. While growing up, he was both an active Boy Scout and Explorer Scout. Morris also enjoyed outdoor activities such as hunting and fishing. With eight mouths to feed, often money was tight for his parents. Still, somehow they were able to send Morris and his siblings to a private school for a few years which provided him with a solid educational foundation. Later however, Morris would return to public school where he continued his thirst for learning. While attending Dunbar High School, he was a free-spirit and well liked student. He enjoyed playing sports but favored baseball above them all.

Military Enlistment

In this small, rural Oklahoma town, there were very few career opportunities, especially for an African-American male. So at the age of 17, Morris decided to give the military a try. He first enlisted in the Oklahoma Army National Guard, 45th Infantry Division. But after just one year, Morris realized he was a good fit for military life and requested a transfer to the United States Army. After having watched a number of family members (including two older brothers) be successful in the military, signing up became an easy decision for him. Along with keeping him out of trouble and letting him travel the world, he hoped the military would provide him with needed skills to enter the workforce after service.

Military Training

Morris went through basic training at Fort Jackson in Columbia, South Carolina. His plan was to follow in the footsteps of an uncle who was a paratrooper. Shortly after completing boot camp, he signed up for jump school. His next advancement would come after hearing about an elite group of soldiers known as the "Green Beret". Also referred to as a Special Forces Group, the Green Beret are highly skilled soldiers who in Vietnam fought using irregular warfare such as ambushes and hit/run missions. Although he was a short young man weighing less than 120 pounds, he was confident that his hard work would make up for his size. So, despite some reservation, he pursued the training and would become one of the first men appointed by President John F. Kennedy to this group of distinguished solders.

Morris Meets His Wife

The military would also influence Morris' personal life. While stationed at Fort Bragg in North Carolina, Morris would meet his bride Mary at a United Service Organization dance. Sergeant Morris and Mary would go on to have three children.

Deployment to Vietnam/Acts of Heroism

One day Morris received notice of deployment to Vietnam. This would be his first tour overseas, and at the young age of 27 with a young wife and children, it proved to be a difficult time for both him and his family. It was during this first tour that Staff Sergeant Morris exhibited great bravery. Serving as leader of the Third Company, after a fellow soldier was shot and killed in a search and destroy mission, Morris and others on his team would go into enemy territory to recover the body. Although he knew this would be a dangerous task, he had too much respect for his brother to leave him there. So he and his team moved toward enemy lines to retrieve the body. When the enemy became aware of their presence, they surrounded the battalion with gunfire. Still, they were able to get the body, but not without injuries.

Dodging bullets and moving as fast as possible, they would make their way through the jungle hoping to get to safety. But, a couple of Morris' men would be shot along the way. This left Morris with the daunting task of having to ensure they got back to base. He had all of this responsibility while still carrying the body of his fallen comrade.

After getting back to camp, Morris remembered that a map had slipped out of the pocket of the fallen soldier. There would be no way he could leave it there because if the enemy were to find it, it might be detrimental to the mission. Although alone, Morris bravely went back into enemy territory to retrieve the lost map. Once he had it, he began to run back to safety. On his way back however, he would encounter gunfire again resulting in his being shot three different times. But with adrenaline flowing and a determination to survive, he used multiple hand grenades to destroy many of the Viet Cong. Later Morris recalls feeling no pain until being medically treated. First he was sent to a hospital in Saigon where he spent a few days. Then he returned home to Fort Bragg, North Carolina where he would have a lengthy recovery. In recognition of his bravery in this act, he received the Distinguished Cross Award in 1970.

Second Tour in Vietnam

Just 30 days later, Staff Sergeant Morris returned to Vietnam to join in the battle once again. Returning to Vietnam for Morris was even more scary the second time. This time he knew what dangers awaited him and his wife now had three children to care for alone. Living on base however, she had a good support system and friends to rely on. Her sisters would also provide lots of assistance in the rearing of the children.

Thankfully Morris returned home safely from his second tour in Vietnam. But to his surprise, only his wife and kids were there to meet him. There was no fanfare and when off base, he discovered some were actually opposed to the United States' involvement in the Vietnam

War. Possibly this would have an influence on his decision to retire just a couple of years after returning from his second tour in Vietnam.

Morris was able to stay away from the military for just three years. Missing the comfort of military life and the feeling he got from service, he opted to reenlist although it meant his starting over at a lower rank. This was the level of dedication and love he had and still has for his country.

Advanced Military Training

Striving to be the best soldier possible, throughout his career, Staff Sergeant Morris participated in both advanced military training and specialty schools. This included engineering school, jump master school, sniper training and air force logistical school. Of all of his training, Morris most enjoyed being a jumpmaster. He liked the thrill that came with jumping out of the plane and the amazing feeling he would get while falling fast toward the earth.

Retirement/Civilian Life

During his career, he also continued as a leader in the Special Force Group. He would spend time stationed at Fort Bragg in North Carolina, and overseas in both Germany and the Dominican Republic. In 1985 during his final assignment at Fort Hood, (Texas) he decided that it was time to retire. At the time of his retirement, he had achieved the rank of Sergeant First Class. After hanging up his uniform, he relocated with his wife to the sunny state of Florida.

Like many, Morris says he struggled with adapting to the civilian world. His family had lived for decades with the support and love of other military families. To his surprise, after leaving the familiarity of military life, Morris began to experience symptoms of post-traumatic stress syndrome. Withdrawn and unable to communicate with others, he became anxious and depressed. Finding employment after a couple of decades in the military also proved to be more of a challenge then he'd originally thought. Morris sought counseling and employment resources through Veterans Affairs which proved extremely helpful. He now works with other veterans to overcome the effects of war.

Call from President Barack Obama

The proudest day for Staff Sergeant Melvin Morris would come years after his military retirement. It was like any other day when Morris got a call from a military official telling him he would be receiving a phone call from an important governmental leader. Morris was excited, but also a little nervous. All kinds of thoughts ran through his mind as to what they'd want to talk to him about. With apprehension, he took another call from the military official the following day as was promised. Morris said he could barely stand when he heard the voice of the 44th president, Barack Obama on the other end of the line. President Obama had called to tell Morris personally of his being selected to receive the Medal of Honor, the highest award one can receive in battle. But he'd have to contain his excitement and keep it a secret until the White House made the announcement.

Official Medal of Honor Ceremony

So on March 18, 2014, Morris and his family arrived at the White House where in an official ceremony, President Barack Obama bestowed upon him the Medal of Honor. It came about because of the work of Congressmen Schumer, Dingell, Mead and Eddie Johnson along with the Black Caucus. These governmental leaders were compelled to reopen files from World War II, Korea and Vietnam. Reviewing over 6,000 military files, their research uncovered many deserving veterans who should have received the distinguished Medal of Honor but didn't due to race or religion. Most had received the Distinguished Service Cross (the second highest designation) much earlier, but on that day they received an upgrade to the highest award – the Medal of Honor.

When interviewed, Staff Sergeant Melvin Morris is not one to brag about his bravery. Instead, he speaks more of the sacrifice that all men and women of the armed forces have made. He also prefers to bring attention to the many men who did not return from war but instead died in battle. His wife, children and siblings however are very proud of him. In truth, they too paid a price for his service being without their husband, brother and father while he was away in Vietnam. Still, this day of honor brought about long overdue recognition for Morris.

Although Morris would receive this commendation at 72 years of age and over 40 years past due, it is a day and honor he will never forget. On this special day, he along with 23 other soldiers had the medal placed around their necks on that cold day in March. Unfortunately, most of the recipients had passed on so a family member stood in their place. Still for many, the tears would flow not because of sadness, but because of joy. Adding to Morris' honor, he was proud that the first African-American President of the United States, Barack Obama, would be the one presenting him with his award.

Each arm of the military has its own distinct Medal of Honor. Crafted of red brass, bronze and gold plating, the Army's Medal of Honor features five pointed stars accented with green oak leafs. An insignia with Staff Sergeant Morris' name is included on the award and engraved on its opposite side. The citation written on the Medal of Honor for Staff Sergeant Melvin Morris reads as follows:

"Staff Sergeant Melvin Morris distinguished himself by acts of gallantry and intrepidity above and beyond the call of duty while serving as Commander of a Strike Force drawn from Company D, 5th Special Forces Group (Airborne), 1st Special Forces, during combat operations against an armed enemy in the vicinity of Chi Lang, Republic of Vietnam on September 17, 1969. On that afternoon, Staff Sergeant Morris' affiliated companies encountered an extensive enemy mine field and were subsequently engaged by a hostile force. Staff Sergeant Morris learned by radio that a fellow team commander had been killed near an enemy bunker and he immediately reorganized his men into an effective assault posture before advancing forward and splitting off with two men to recover the team commander's body. Observing the maneuver, the hostile force

concentrated its fire on Staff Sergeant Morris' three-man element and successfully wounded both men accompanying him. After assisting the two wounded men back to his forces' lines, Staff Sergeant Morris charged forward into withering enemy fire with only his men's suppressive fire as cover. While enemy machine gun emplacements continuously directed strafing fusillades against him, Staff Sergeant Morris destroyed the positions with hand grenades and continued his assault, ultimately eliminating four bunkers. Upon reaching the bunker nearest the fallen team commander, Staff Sergeant Morris repulsed the enemy, retrieved his comrade and began the arduous trek back to friendly lines. He was wounded three times as he struggled forward, but ultimately succeeded in returning his fallen comrade to a friendly position. Staff Sergeant Morris' extraordinary heroism and selflessness above and beyond the call of duty are in keeping with the highest traditions of military service and reflect great credit upon himself, his unit, and the United States Army."

Other Awards and Designations

Along with the Medal of Honor and Distinguished Cross Award, Morris is also the recipient of the Bronze Star, Purple Heart, National Defense Service Medal and the Meritorious Award. His skill level and dedication to professionalism is also confirmed by the many accolades and training medals he has received including the Master Parachutist, Experts Marksmanship and the Combat Infantryman Badge. Additionally, he has been inducted in the Oklahoma Military Hall of Fame and the Pentagon Hall of Heroes and his name engraved on the wall of the Special Operations Memorial at MacDill Air Force Base in Florida. Numerous community organizations have also honored him including the Melbourne Regional Chamber of Commerce and Okmulgee Lions Club.

Life after the Medal of Honor/Work with Veterans

When asked if he would change anything about his past, Morris says he would not. In spite of the injuries and horrors of war, Staff Sergeant Morris loves freedom and his country. He says he is humbled to be a recipient of the Medal of Honor. He says receiving this esteemed award has changed his life by making him a hero to the nation. From it, he has developed even more of a commitment to helping others. Consequently, Morris has accepted numerous invitations to speak at schools, churches and special events. When speaking, he is happy to talk about his experiences in Vietnam. But most often he will talk about the mental trauma and rehabilitation needs of veterans following war. He especially enjoys talking with youth about freedom, its cost and the responsibilities of future generations. Some of Morris' speaking engagements have included his being the featured speaker at the Spirit of America Leaders Youth Summit Gala held in 2016, the Marine Corp League's Medal of Honor Day in Tulsa and the seminar speaker for the Oklahoma ROTC in August of 2016. He has also spoken at various schools around the country including high schools in the Minneapolis (Minnesota), Columbia (South Carolina) and Concord (Massachusetts) areas.

Since his receiving the Medal of Honor, colleges, universities and communities have also developed scholarships to continue the legacy of excellence Morris began a few decades ago. A couple of these include the University of Montana's Melvin S. Morris Award and the Gala Funds Scholarship for Spirit of America Leaders.

Although long-delayed, after attending the White House celebration, other veterans, citizens and organizations want to continue to celebrate the bravery of Staff Sergeant Morris. One such honor and recognition came from the Washington Nationals in 2014. At its season opener against the Atlanta Braves, Morris was called to the mound to throw out the ceremonial pitch. Both nervous and anxious, he just hoped to get the ball to the catcher. He'd been practicing with his grandson since the phone call but was still not that confident. Nonetheless, he had a good throw and after the pitch, walked off the field to a standing ovation and massive cheers from the crowd. Morris attended the game with his family including his wife Mary and a grandson who is a huge baseball fan.

Another proud day for Morris took place in the nearby Florida town of Cocoa. Displayed in the city's Riverfront Park, there is a bronze, life size statue of Morris for all park goers to see. A project of the Civilian Military Community Foundation, it includes a plaque that educates the public about Staff Sergeant Melvin Morris and the reasons for him being a Medal of Honor Recipient. Morris and his family attended a ceremony in May of 2015. He actually removed the shroud and presented the statue to the community which he says "gave him an eerie feeling."

Morris' Life Today

Today Morris lives a quiet life in a small, suburban town in Florida. He resides with his wife of over 50 years and their beloved dog Lucky. The proud father of three adult children, one daughter and two sons (one of which served in the Army and another the Air Force), Morris is now enjoying being a grandfather and most recently a great-grandfather. During his free time, he likes to fish and boat with friends, and when looking to relax, goes outdoors to groom his garden and play in the dirt. Continuing to strive to serve others, he is also active in his church and serves as an advocate for veterans of wars in Vietnam, Iraq and Afghanistan. Morris proudly displays his Medal of Honor and other military achievements throughout his home for family members and visitors to see. He also flies the United States flag outside of his home daily to show his continued respect and pride in this country. As often as he can, he continues to travel the states speaking about his courageous acts and encouraging the youth. Morris will forever be a hero to his fellow veterans, community and family.

David Dolby

When an active duty member of the U.S military is awarded the Medal of Honor, that soldier, sailor, Marine or airman is usually given an assignment far from the battlefield until their tour of duty or time in the service has ended. During World War II, Medal of Honor recipients were utilized on bond drives and recruitment tours. The armed forces, realizing both that these men (to this date, only one woman has won the Medal of Honor, and that was during the Civil War) have gone far above the call of duty and can potentially be more away from the battlefield than on it usually only reluctantly allows Medal of Honor winners to serve in combat once again.

The most well-known case of a Medal of Honor winner returning to combat is that of WWII Marine Gunnery Sergeant John Basilone (1916-1945). Awarded the nations' highest citation for his actions in the defense of a vital position in the early stages of the Battle of Guadalcanal in 1942, Basilone returned to a heroes' welcome in the United States. Among the nations first World War II heroes, Basilone was given parades, took part in bond tours, appeared in newsreels urging men to join the Marines and for American's to contribute to the war effort with all they had.

Basilone (who had already served in the Army before joining the Marines in 1940) did not adjust well to life "stateside", despite his happy marriage to Marine Reserve Sergeant Lena Mae Riggi. He refused promotion and an assignment as an instructor, and pushed for reinstatement for active front line duty, which was finally granted in time for the run up to the invasion of Iwo Jima in February 1945. It was there while leading his men on an assault on a Japanese position that Basilone was killed by enemy fire. Just over twenty years later, a Medal of Honor winner named David Dolby voluntarily returned to combat in Vietnam.

In 1964, when David Dolby first joined the US Army, the United States was becoming more and more involved in the war between communist North Vietnam and pro-Western South Vietnam. Vietnam had been a French colonial possession from the late 19th century onward, but after the disaster of WWII and its defeat by the forces of the Vietnamese communists at Dien Bien Phu in 1954, France relinquished control of its possessions in Southeast Asia. By agreement, Vietnam was split into two nations, and it was hoped by the French that the United States would support the new anti-Communist government in the South, based in Saigon (today's Ho Chi Minh City).

By the late 1950's and early 1960's, the United States had been involved in a political and ideological battle with the communist Soviet Union (and its ally the People's Republic of China) for over a decade. In the minds of politicians of both sides, inroads by the other side anywhere in the world had to be countered by the other. Politicians from both parties as well as the bulk of the American people viewed any gains by Soviet sponsored communism as a defeat and a threat and were determined to counter any communist moves with military, political and economic maneuvers of their own.

Though the Treaty of Paris which ended French involvement in Vietnam was supposed to secure peace between the new nations of North and South Vietnam, no one really believed that the forces of the North would stop fighting for the unification of Vietnam under communism. By the early 1960's, an increasingly intense civil war had developed between the North and South.

Supplying the North with weapons, equipment, money and advisers were the Soviets and the Chinese. Conversely, the United States supplied and supported the South. Facing each other on the battlefield were the North Vietnamese Army ("NVA") and the guerrillas of the National Liberation Front (better known by their Vietnamese name: "Viet Cong" - "VC" to the Americans) against the South's Army of the Republic of Vietnam ("ARVN") and their American advisers.

From the late 1950's and especially after the election of President John F. Kennedy in 1960, US involvement in Vietnam had steadily increased. In 1963, most of the American troops in South Vietnam were Army Special Forces (better known then as the "Green Berets"). By 1965, events both military and political had led to a massive escalation in US involvement in the country. In 1963 there were some 16,000 men US servicemen in Vietnam. By 1966 when David Dolby arrived "in-country", there were nearly 400,000.

David was born in the small city of Norristown, Pennsylvania on May 14, 1946 to Charles (a WWII veteran and POW) and Mary Dolby. Mary and Charles also had a younger son named Daniel. At Spring Ford High School, David was on both the football and wrestling teams – his brother called him "the toughest guy in three counties". Upon graduation, David almost immediately went to the local recruiting center and enlisted in the US Army. By the time he entered the army David was a solid and muscular six feet tall.

In 1964-65 when David joined the army, most Americans, while perhaps not rabid supporters of the war, felt that America's interest in Southeast Asia was warranted. It did not take long for these opinions to change, and by the late 1960's and early 1970's more and more

Americans were urging both the Johnson and later, the Nixon administrations to end our involvement there.

When Americans look back on the 1960's today in relation to the Vietnam War through documentaries and movies we are bombarded with images of anti-war demonstrators and activists demanding that the US government end its involvement in Vietnam. There is no mistaking that as time went by the anti-war movement grew in strength. Many Americans began to see that the war was un-winnable, that perhaps the United States did not have vital interests in Vietnam, and that the war was at the center of much of the strife that was beginning to tear the nation apart.

We must remember two things however. First, opposition to the war, while always vocal, was not as popular then as it might seem now – especially in 1964-67 when force levels increased and many believed the war was winnable. Second, not all, but much of the anti-war movement and its support came from large urban centers, colleges and on the coasts. In the American heartland and in small towns and rural areas such as Norristown, Pennsylvania, support for the war was much stronger.

From 1940 to 1972, American men were drafted for military service. In time of war, the numbers of those drafted increased. Though the number of those drafted reached over two million during the Vietnam War, during the conflict (from 1964-75) over eight million men were stationed in Vietnam at one time or another. Most of those men did not see combat.

Still, hundreds of thousands of Americans in Vietnam were draftees and many of them did not want to be there. Hundreds of thousands more get deferments of one kind or another. Full-time college students were not drafted (among the many factors contributing to the accusation that the poor fought overseas while the rich stayed home (the economically backward state of West Virginia saw the highest percentage of deaths per population), many married men (especially those with children) were exempt, those with serious criminal convictions were also not drafted, as well as those with jobs considered vital to the "national interest". Medical reasons also kept many out of the military. Pressure on local doctors for a deferment letter was great. Of course, the men who garnered the most notoriety were those who fled the country to avoid the draft (most of these one hundred thousand men were pardoned by President Gerald Ford in 1974). Most of those sent to Vietnam did not see combat and were well away from the battlefield.

Still, despite all of the news stories, demonstrations, and lack of wholehearted support for the war, many more men enlisted rather than wait for the draft. Many of those from poor backgrounds joined in order to perhaps further themselves. Many just wanted to get out of their rural or small town lives. Some wanted to get away from family or sought adventure. During the war years, about 25% of those who served in Vietnam were drafted. The rest were career military or enlisted themselves (either out of a sense of duty or to beat the draft). About 30% of the Americans killed in Vietnam were draftees (almost 18,000).

David Dolby's father was a veteran of WWII, and had imbued both his sons' with the importance of duty and service, and that combined with a desire to challenge himself compelled David to enlist in the Army before he could be drafted and perhaps sent to a branch of the service in which he had no interest.

By all accounts, David Dolby was a tough, athletic young man who yearned to prove himself. At the beginning of 1966, David left for Vietnam, joining with what would become one of the most famous American units of the Vietnam War, the 1st Cavalry (Airmobile). The 1st Cavalry (or "1st Air Cav") was involved in some of the most intense fighting of the war from the moment they were deployed to Vietnam in 1965. The division was commanded by General Harold "Harry" Kinnard, who had come to the attention of command for his role as

General Anthony McAuliffe's aide during the Battle of the Bulge in WWII (it was Kinnard that suggested that McAuliffe's comment of "Nuts!" to a German surrender command be the reply the Americans gave the Nazis).

The first major engagement fought by the 1st was in the heavily forested the Ia Drang river valley east of the provincial South Vietnamese city of Plei Me near the Cambodian border. The book "We Were Soldiers Once, and Young" by Harold Moore and Joseph Galloway and the subsequent Mel Gibson movie (2002) "We Were Soldiers" were based on this battle. Over 300 hundred American and South Vietnamese soldiers were killed and an estimated 1,000 NVA soldiers were killed during the four day battle. In May, 1966 Dolby was a member of the 1st AirCav's 8th Cavalry Regiment, 1st Battalion, Company "B" commanded by Captain Roy D. Martin. Dolby's platoon commander was Lieutenant Robert H. Crum.

By the time David Dolby joined with the 1st Air Cav, the division had already seen its first action and many of its men were combat veterans. As a newly arrived and green Specialist 4 (a rank which does not exist in today's US Army, but can be roughly compared to a corporal), Dolby was likely given some of the more unpleasant tasks in camp in addition to his responsibility as his squads' machine gunner.

In his account of his time in Vietnam, *Forsaken Warriors: The Story of an American Advisor who Fought with the South Vietnamese Rangers and Airborne,* Robert Tonsetic speaks of running into (then sergeant) David Dolby on one of Dolby's later tours of duty: "Dolby was a bit of a loner, and spent hours stripping and cleaning the team's M-60 machine guns. Sergeant Roberts told me later that Dolby would walk point for the entire 400-man Ranger battalion armed with the M-60..."

Tonsetic's account is from 1969, three years after the action which resulted in Dolby's being awarded the Medal of Honor. Perhaps the Dolby of 1969 was a war weary veteran who had seen a number of his comrades die and wished to remain as aloof as possible, but most people who knew the man give accounts of a friendly, but reserved man, before and after the war. Many years later, his brother Daniel spoke of David as someone who was able to talk about his war-time experiences despite the pain the memories sometimes engendered. "You could see the pain in his eyes, but he would chuckle. . . . He wasn't fractured."

Three years earlier, David carried the M-60 machine gun into combat during Operation Crazy Horse. Still in use today, the M-60 is generally (but not always) handled by a three man crew. Though the weapon is light enough (for a machine gun) to be fired by one man, its high rate of fire often requires a support team carrying extra ammunition, and parts such as spare barrels. At times the second or even a third man will function as a spotter. However, in many circumstances the machine gun can be successfully and effectively operated by one man - provided he is strong and in shape. David Dolby was one such man. In Vietnam, many Navy SEAL's and Special Forces machine gunners carried modified M-60's cut down to reduce weight and a number of special forces operatives carried customized backpacks with much extra ammunition, fed directly into the weapon to avoid reloading at crucial moments.

The gun has undergone many improvements and iterations, but is still very much like the first model that came off factory floors in 1957. The weapon fires a 7.62 NATO round and has a rate of fire of 500-50 rounds per minute. It's effective range is about 1,000 yards, but in Vietnam this was usually not needed.

The M-60 was loved by the men it protected – it gave an infantry squad firepower out of proportion to its numbers, but it was prone to breakdowns, especially if it was not meticulously maintained. During heavy firing the weapon was prone to jamming, especially if it was dirty. On patrol in the jungles, forest and rice paddies of Vietnam, when it might not be possible to keep the weapon in pristine condition, mud and debris could combine with gun grease and powder to cause the weapon to break down. The trigger mechanism could sometimes be faulty, resulting in gunner's having to jury rig the mechanism to ensure proper firing. The latch that allowed the barrel to be switched out quickly was located in an odd spot and sometimes hooked on a gunners clothing or equipment, which resulted in the barrel dropping off unexpectedly. When barrels did need to be changed, protective hand gear was necessary to protect the gunner/crews hands from the red-hot barrel, and additionally, the weapon had another serious design flaw when used in Vietnam – the barrel did not come off by itself. Its attached bi-pod came off with it. When firing from a prone position, the gunner or his assistant had no handle by which to remove the barrel – and they had to raise up from a prone position to allow the barrel and bi-pod to come off. Needless to say, a kneeling man is much more of a target than one lying prone.

Despite all of this, however, a gunner with strength and an eye for detail (such as David Dolby) could operate the weapon *very* effectively.

When David joined the 1st AirCav, the unit was reinforcing and resupplying between assignments. Already mentioned is the famous action in the Ia Drang Valley in 1965. In early 1966, the division took part in "Operation Masher", in Binh Dinh province, located on the central coast of Vietnam (the northern part of South Vietnam). According to intelligence reports, the province was virtually under the control of the NVA and Viet Cong, and was a vital area for the transfer of northern forces and supplies southward, as well as an important communications and intelligence center. Operation Masher, which was the largest "search and destroy" operation up to that time, involved the 1st AirCav, South Vietnamese units and units from South Korea (a nation which provided a substantial force to the American effort in Vietnam).

Over the course of a few weeks, the Americans and their allies inflicted heavy losses on the NVA and Viet Cong, but suffered some three hundred dead and an additional large number of wounded. The "search and destroy" aspect of the Vietnam War has came under great criticism during the war and since – units would seek out and attack known enemy formations, and then eventually evacuate the area, only to see the Viet Cong gradually reassert themselves among the villages and forests. It was during the tail end of Operation Masher that David Dolby gained his first experiences in the field. By .late spring, he was a veteran, and one who was recognized as having a singular coolness in the field and amazing strength.

Operation Masher had destroyed a number of Viet Cong and NVA units but had not succeeded in eliminating Viet Cong influence in the province. The Viet Cong 2nd Regiment of some 2,000 men (and women) was thought to be in the area, and that was multifaceted threat – the enemy could cut the vital Route 19 to the south, threaten both 1st AirCav outposts near the town of An He and an anti-Viet Cong Vietnamese counter-insurgency group supported by the Americans.

The enemy was thought to be concentrated in two valleys to the west of An Khe. The Vinh Thanh valley nearest the town of An Khe and the base of the 1st AirCav was small, but presented a number of problems. First, it was densely populated – which meant that the guerrilla Viet Cong might be able to blend into the population. Second, despite its heavy population, the valley was heavily forested and bordered by high hills, which provided excellent cover and possibilities for fortification. The valley was some twelve miles long and just three miles wide.

Southeast of the Vinh Thanh valley was Suoi Ca Valley, a smaller area but heavily forested. In between the two valleys was a high spur of hills which overlooked both areas. It was there that the 1st AirCav positioned itself in an effort to cut off and remove the Viet Cong threat to the area.

There are a number of accounts of the actions that took place during Operation Crazy Horse. The most famous is that of famous military historian S.L.A Marshall who wrote of the battle just a few years after it had occurred. However, there are discrepancies in the accounts of Marshall and a number of officers that were on scene. The "B" company commander, Captain Roy Martin has written his own account of the action (for which he was awarded the Distinguished Service Cross), and disputes a number of Marshall's assertions, primarily those recounting close artillery and air support supposedly called in by himself and other officers during the height of the battle. Martin states that the fighting took place in such close quarters that any American artillery or air attacks would have resulted in friendly fire. Martin requested artillery twice that day – once as the men of his company approached suspected VC positions a distance away, and one other time a bit later, before the battle proper began, when he was told that the guns were unavailable – they were relocating to another position. Martin also disputes Marshall's assertion that he personally spoke with Sergeant Dolby on the day Dolby won his Medal of Honor. What Martin does not deny is that Dolby deserved the nations' highest citation for his actions on May 21, 1966.

Three battalions of the 1st took position on the spur that separated the Vinh Thanh from the Suoi Ca valleys over the course of May 16 to 20. One battalion of the 12th Cavalry remained in reserve at their highland base further to the east. The Americans had three "LZ's" (landing zones) on the spur separating the valleys. Furthest west was LZ Hereford. Slightly northeast was LZ Monkey, and to the southeast was LZ Horse. Approximately two miles to the west across a small river near the village of Dinh Binh was LZ Savoy, the location of the Vietnamese anti-insurgent group and a number of American Special Forces operators, as well as members of the 1st AirCav's "I" Company.

This last group was meant to be a blocking force intercepting any enemy formations attempting to retreat westward.

The American landing zones and concentration area formed a triangular shape about 2 miles long and less than a mile wide. The US forces were concentrated for maximum effect and it was hoped that a high degree of coordination could be achieved to root out the Viet Cong, who were dug into positions throughout the valley and in adjoining hills. Running east/west through the Suoi Ca valley was a small trail (dubbed the "Oregon Trail" by the 1st AirCav) which was used by the enemy for movement and supply.

At 1600 hours (4 PM) on May 20, B Company boarded three Chinook (CH-47) took off for LZ Horse overlooking the two strategic valleys of Vinh Thanh and Suoi Ca. On each of the dual-rotor helicopters were 40 men and their supplies. Among them was David Dolby. Flying at nine thousand feet, the men on the Chinooks could clearly see the forests, villages and valleys below them as they approached the LZ – the weather was clear and mild. Coming in from the south, Captain Martin and the helicopter pilots could see the Vietnamese/Special Forces camp to the east of the large stream/small river that separated them from the main landing zones. To the right of the choppers is a waterfall coming out of the heavily forested mountains near the LZ.

Landing Zone Horse was not an elaborate airfield – far from it. LZ Horse and the other landing zones were small clearings (about 25 yards by 25 yards) cut from the high elephant grass of the area. In the case of Horse, the field was bisected by a small stream. As Martin and the men of B Company began their approach, they could see cooking fires in the hills – Martin knew these were Viet Cong positions.

Each Chinook in turn hovered above the small field at about ten feet. In ten to fifteen seconds, the forty men on board and their supplies were on the ground and moving into position on the perimeter of the LZ. In about one minute the entire company was on the ground.

Before darkness fell, the men of the company had established defensive positions. The men settled in as best they could, knowing that in all likelihood they would be in combat the next day – if not before, for by this time, the Americans were beginning to realize that the VC were masters in night-time warfare. As luck would have it the Vietnamese did not attack that evening, and the men spent the remaining daylight hours attending their equipment and in the many private thoughts that run through a soldier's mind before combat.

Unlike the previous day, the 21st dawned hot and humid with little wind. At 0700 the next morning the men of B Company moved out into the thick forest which covered the hills above the Suoi Ca valley. The were to move to the south of the stream which bisected LZ Horse and move eastward to rendezvous with "C" Company, which would be moving to the north of the stream.

At about 1100 hours 2nd Platoon of "B" Company came under fire from enemy machine guns, wounding one man, who had to wait while his comrades constructed a litter out of tree branches and their ponchos before they were able to carry him back to LZ Horse for later evacuation. Captain Martin knew that his unit had run into the first outposts of what would prove to be a series of heavily fortified enemy positions. The suspected enemy positions were then taken care of by the aforementioned single artillery barrage of the morning.

As the men of "B" Company advanced, they saw more and more evidence that a large member of Viet Cong had been in the area, and just shortly before the Americans' arrival. Smoking campfires, well-traveled trails, bamboo tables and assorted garbage told the men of "B" that the enemy was very close indeed.

By this time, the men had entered extremely heavy forest, the sun partially blocked out by the canopy above. This combined with the hilly terrain made it difficult to keep contact with their comrades in other companies, and caused Captain Martin and his men to be very cautious, not only because they knew the enemy was near, but because of the danger of a friendly-fire incident. As they slowly moved into the canopy, Martin felt it was time to rendezvous with the commander of the nearest friendly unit, Captain Bill Mosey. Martin's men did their best to form a defensive position while their CO met with his counter-part from "C". At 1400 hours, over a shared tin of jelly and some crackers, the two officers decided on their next move - "C" Company would neutralize a series of enemy bunkers that were on their side of the stream separating the American units. Mosey and his men had already engaged and killed a number of the enemy, and were preparing to chase the rest back into what they assumed was a fortified position. While "C" was doing this, "B" would move to the south and attempt to flank the enemy position, which was now assumed to be battalion strength.

It was at this time that Martin called in the artillery mission that could not be completed because the guns were being re-positioned. He wanted to lay down a barrage on the hill immediately to his company's front, having not only seen enemy troops moving through the forest, but knowing that the likelihood of there being Viet Cong bunkers on the hill being high.

At about 1600 hours, the men of "B" Company were moving through the positions of "C", forming a "V" on the slopes and base of the hill. First Platoon was to Martin's right and behind him about fifty yards on the slope of the hill when they came under heavy enemy machine gun fire from both medium and large caliber enemy machine guns. Martin's command location was also being fired at, but due to the nature of the terrain, this fire went far over the heads of the men in Martin's retinue. First Platoon was not so lucky. Martin attempted to reach the First Platoon commander, Lieutenant Robert Crum Jr., but could not reach him. Martin did not know it at the time, but First Platoon and its commander were now taking heavy casualties – and that's when David Dolby of Norristown, Pennsylvania sprang into action.

As they slowly advanced up the hill, First Platoon came under intense enemy machine gun fire which instantly killed six men of the squad on point. Among them, attempting to assess the situation was Lt. Crum, who was also hit. Watching all of this happen was David Dolby, who through a miracle of fate was unscathed.

When Crum went down, Dolby ran and pulled him to cover. The lieutenant, who likely knew he was dying (he passed shortly afterward), told Dolby to Take over, and get the men out of here." Immediately Dolby began to lay down covering fire on the enemy positions, moving from rock to rock and tree to tree seeking cover while he he yelled to the men of the platoon to pull back. As they did, Dolby laid down heavy fire to cover their withdrawal. As he moved from one firing position to another, enemy machine gun fire trailed him, chewing up the trees, dirt and stumps around him.

As the men came down from the hill closer to Dolby's position, and while he was both under fire and firing on the enemy (and neutralizing one position after another), Dolby ordered the able-bodied to defensive positions and directed their fire. As if this was not enough for one man to accomplish while under heavy enemy fire, Dolby assisted wounded men coming down off the hill.

It must also be remembered that Dolby was carrying a twnety0five pound machine gun and its ammunition single-handedly. A number of times over the course of a *four hour* battle, Dolby ran back to his unit's main position and replenished his ammunition. When he did, he sprinted back up the hill and carried on his attack.

As the afternoon progressed, David Dolby killed another three enemy machine gunners, and neutralized much of the enemy fire coming down on his men. This also allowed the other platoons of "B" Company, under the direction of Martin and their platoon commanders, to work their way around the enemy positions from their place at the bottom of the hill.

A number of times, Dolby marked enemy positions with smoke grenades for air strikes and mortar barrages. Additionally Dolby repeatedly assaulted other enemy positions that day, taking out enemy snipers and and support troops. All through the afternoon, Dolby both assaulted the enemy, assisted wounded men and helped the rest of his unit move into stronger defensive positions. He both directed the action and performed much of it for four long hours. By the time the day ended, the remainder of "B" Company, along with "C" had neutralized the enemy strong points and taken their positions. For his part in the actions that day, David Dolby was awarded the Silver Star, which was upgraded to the Medal of Honor, which was presented to him by President Johnson in the White House in 1967.

As was mentioned in the first part of this paper, Dolby was returned home and given duty training other troops, but this was not what Dolby was meant for. In 1967 he pushed for a return to duty in Vietnam and served with the illustrious 101st Airborne. In 1969 he joined "C" Company of the 75th Rangers and in 1970 went back again, this time as an adviser to the Royal Cambodian Army. When he left the army, he had, besides the Medal of Honor and Silver Star, been awarded the Purple Heart.

David married a Vietnamese wife, Xuan, but did not have any children. In the early 1970's, Dolby went through a rough time trying to adjust to civilian life. During a vacation in Florida, he passed a number of bad checks in small amounts, probably just to keep the party going a little longer. Arrested, he was given probation – his service to the nation probably saved him from jail time. Unfortunately, the obituaries for David that one finds on the Internet carry headlines about this one small isolated incident in Dolby's life. He was a young man, who made a mistake, and though civilian life after the war was not necessarily easy for David (he held a series of blue collar jobs and at times battled PTSD), he was not an outlaw. He was a young man trying to find his way after performing deeds and seeing things that most men can not even dream of.

Though he spent the rest of his life in relative anonymity, Dolby spent much of his time working with other veterans, making speeches to civic groups and attending other veterans' events. When he died in 2010, he was at a retreat in Idaho, having given a speech to a veterans group and having a good time with his comrades.